ISEE Upper Level Practice Tests

ISEE Upper Level Practice Tests

Three Full-Length Verbal and Quantitative
Mock Tests with Detailed Answer Explanations

ANTHEM PRESS

Anthem Press
An imprint of Wimbledon Publishing Company
www.anthempress.com

This edition first published in UK and USA 2023
by ANTHEM PRESS
75–76 Blackfriars Road, London SE1 8HA, UK
or PO Box 9779, London SW19 7ZG, UK
and
244 Madison Ave #116, New York, NY 10016, USA

© Accel Learning LLC www.accellearning.com 2023

ISEE is not involved in the publication of this book and does not endorse or sponsor this work.

The author asserts the moral right to be identified as the author of this work.

British Library Cataloguing-in-Publication Data
A catalogue record for this book is available from the British Library.

Library of Congress Control Number: 2023936663
A catalog record for this book has been requested.

ISBN-13: 978-1-83998-986-5 (Pbk)
ISBN-10: 1-83998-986-6 (Pbk)

This title is also available as an e-book.

Contents

ISEE Overview

About ISEE

What is the ISEE?

What is ISEE? The Independent School Entrance Examination (ISEE) is an exam created and administered by the Educational Records Bureau (ERB). It tests students' individual academic achievements and reasoning skills as a basis for admission to private schools in the United States and internationally. The ISEE is the admission test of choice for many independent schools throughout the country and abroad.

The ISEE has five sections (in order of testing): Verbal Reasoning, Quantitative Reasoning, Reading Comprehension and Vocabulary, Mathematics Achievement, and an Essay which is written by the student in response to a given writing prompt. Each section is designed to tap into a unique aspect of a student's preparation for academic work. The first four sections consist entirely of multiple-choice questions.

How does a student arrange to take the ISEE?

Students may take the ISEE in one of the following ways:

1. The ISEE is given at individual school test sites at a wide variety of schools throughout the country and abroad and on a number of test dates.

2. The ISEE can also be given at the ERB office in New York and at offices in other parts of the country, visit: www.erblearn.org for more details.

What types of questions are on the ISEE?

The first four sections are composed of multiple-choice questions. The fifth section, the essay, is not scored but requires the student to respond to a preselected writing prompt.

The first two sections, **Verbal Reasoning** and **Quantitative Reasoning**, measure the applicant's reasoning ability.

The **Verbal Reasoning** test consists of two types of items: vocabulary and sentence completion.

At the Lower Level, the **Quantitative Reasoning** test consists of word problems.

The next two sections, **Reading Comprehension and Vocabulary** and **Mathematics Achievement,** measure the applicant's ability to correctly answer curriculum-based concepts that are appropriate at that grade level.

In order to determine a student's reading comprehension skills, in the Reading Comprehension and Vocabulary section, the student is asked to read a passage and then answer items specific to that passage.

Mathematics Achievement items conform to national mathematics standards and ask the student to identify the problem and find a solution to a problem. The items require one or more steps in calculating the answer.

The **Essay** is written by the student in response to a writing "prompt" or topic that is grade-level appropriate. The prompts rotate throughout the testing season. They are designed to prompt a student to write an informed essay on a particular topic.

The table below gives a quick snapshot of the questions in the ISEE.

Test Section	Questions	Time	Details
Verbal Reasoning	40–34	20 minutes	Tests vocabulary and reasoning abilities Synonym section focuses on word recognition Sentence Completion section measures students' knowledge of words and their function Use context clues to decide which word best fits the sentence
Quantitative Reasoning	38–37	35 minutes	Tests mathematical synthesis, skill, comprehension, and logical reasoning Quantitative Reasoning problems are higher-order thinking problems Interpreting data Solving application problems Estimating Recognizing patterns Solving nonroutine problems
Reading Comprehension and Vocabulary	36–25	35–25 minutes	Tests reading ability through six to eight passages, depending on the ISEE test level Each passage is followed by at least four text-related questions
Mathematics Achievement	47–30	40–30 minutes	Correlates with common mathematics curriculum taught in schools Students may NOT use calculators on the ISEE
Essay	1	30 minutes	Students' essays must be in response to a provided prompt Students' essays are sent to each school that receives the ISEE score report Essays are NOT SCORED, but are instead evaluated individually by each school The ISEE essay section is intended for students to demonstrate their writing abilities

How will this book help me?

This book is structured just like the real ISEE. As you practice the tests given in this book, it will help you with:

- Building confidence.
- Getting clarity on the topics.
- Building knowledge about the ISEE.
- Understanding your strengths and weaknesses.
- Becoming familiar with the test layout, structure, and level of difficulty.

ISEE Test Taking

Why should one take the ISEE?

The school you are applying to has requested ISEE scores as part of the overall admissions process. By requiring an admission test for all students entering the same grade, the school can view one common item of all applicants. The school looks at many items in conjunction with the ISEE scores, including your application, your current school records, and possibly an interview. All components of the admission process, including the ISEE scores, help the school, you, and your family determine the best school match for you.

How many times can I take the ISEE?

The ISEE may be taken only when making a formal application to a school(s). You may take the ISEE only once per admission season, and you may not take the ISEE for practice.

What can I expect at the test site on the day of the test?

Students will present their verification letter or identification to be checked in upon arrival. They will be directed to the testing room. They will be provided with the testing material and other supplies. Although test administrators may not discuss test questions during the test, they give clear test directions, and you are encouraged to ask for clarification, if necessary, before beginning each section of the test.

Are there any scheduled breaks during the test?

There are two breaks—one following the Quantitative Reasoning section and another following the Mathematics Achievement section. Each break is 5 minutes long.

What materials do I need to bring to the actual ISEE?

Students should bring four #2 pencils and two pens with either blue or black ink. Students may choose to use erasable ink.

Are there materials that are prohibited from using during the ISEE?

Scrap paper, calculators, smartwatches, rulers, protractors, compasses, dictionaries, and cell phones are NOT permitted during the actual test.

Is there penalty for a wrong answer? Can I guess?

There is no penalty for a wrong answer, but it is not advised to guess.

ISEE Results

What happens to my scores?

After you take the ISEE and your answer sheet is scored, ERB will send copies of the scores and the essay you wrote to the schools that you have chosen, within 7–10 business days. They will send a copy of your test scores (but not a copy of the essay) to your family.

How is the essay scored?

The essay is not scored. However, a copy is sent to the school(s) to which a student sends score reports as indicated on the registration. Evaluation is based on each individual school's criteria.

How soon will I receive my scores?

Students will receive the scores in 7–10 business days.

What is the raw score?

A raw score represents the number correct. If a student got 35 items correct—say on a test of 40 questions—then the raw score is simply 35.

What is the scaled score?

Scaled score is a raw score that has been converted to a different numerical scale, e.g., 200–800. The raw score scale ranges from 0 to maximum score, while the scaled score range consists of higher numbers with a somewhat arbitrary minimum and maximum score. The range of scaled scores on the ISEE is 760–940.

What is the percentile score?

A percentile score is a relative score compared to other independent school applicants who have applied to the same grade during the past three years.

The percentile ranking helps private schools compare a student's performance with others in their applicant cohorts. **The higher your percentile, the better your ISEE score.** For example, a 45th percentile ranking means that the student scored the same as or better than 45% of students in the last three years.

What is a stanine?

A stanine score is simply another scale and is based on percentile ranks. Percentile ranks range from 1 to 99, while stanines range from 1 to 9. In general, a stanine score of 1–3 is below average, 4–6 is average, and 7–9 is above average.

How will I know if I passed or failed?

Students do not pass or fail the ISEE. There is no cutoff point that determines pass/fail status or divides students into these two groups. There is no cutoff (or pass/fail) score recommended by ERB.

ISEE—Upper Level Exam-1

Introduction

The **Independent School Entrance Exam (ISEE Exam)** is a school entrance exam taken by students in grades 4–12 seeking admission into private schools and non-Catholic religious schools throughout the United States. The Upper Level ISEE Exam is for students currently in grades 8–11 who are candidates for admission to grades 9–12.

The ISEE is an admission test that has three levels: A Lower Level, Middle Level, and Upper Level. The Lower Level is for students currently in grades 4 and 5 who are candidates for admission to grades 5 and 6. The Middle Level is for students in grades 6 and 7 who are candidates for grades 7 and 8. The Upper Level is for students in grades 8–11 who are candidates for grades 9–12.

Summary

Who can take the test?	Students from grades 8 through 11			
When is the test conducted?	Students may register to take the ISEE one time in any or all of three testing seasons. The ISEE testing seasons are defined as Fall (August–November), Winter (December–March), and Spring/Summer (April–July)			
What is the format of the test?	All questions are multiple choice			
What is the medium of the test?	Paper based			
What are the topics covered in the test?	**Test Section**	**Questions**	**Time**	**Details**
	Verbal Reasoning	40–34	20 minutes	Tests vocabulary and reasoning abilities Synonym section focuses on word recognition Sentence Completion section measures students' knowledge of words and their function Use context clues to decide which word best fits the sentence
	Quantitative Reasoning	38–37	35 minutes	Tests mathematical synthesis, skill, comprehension, and logical reasoning Quantitative Reasoning problems are higher-order thinking problems Interpreting data Solving application problems Estimating Recognizing patterns Solving nonroutine problems
	Reading Comprehension and Vocabulary	36–25	35–25 minutes	Tests reading ability through six to eight passages, depending on the ISEE test level Each passage is followed by at least four text-related questions

(Continued)

(Continued)

	Mathematics Achievement	47–30	40–30 minutes	Correlates with common mathematics curriculum taught in schools Students may NOT use calculators on the ISEE
	Essay	1	30 minutes	Students' essays must be in response to a provided prompt Students' essays are sent to each school that receives the ISEE score report Essays are NOT SCORED, but are instead evaluated individually by each school The ISEE essay section is intended for students to demonstrate their writing abilities
How long is the test?	Depending on the level, the actual testing time is between **2 hours and 20 minutes to 2 hours and 40 minutes.**			

Verbal Reasoning

You have 20 minutes to answer the 40 questions in the Verbal Reasoning Section.

This section is divided into two parts that contain two different types of questions. As soon as you have completed Part I, answer the questions in Part II. You may write in your test booklet. For each answer you select, fill in the corresponding circle on your answer document.

Part I—Synonyms

Each question in Part I consists of a word in capital letters followed by four answer choices. Select the one word that is most nearly the same in meaning as the word in capital letters.

SAMPLE QUESTION:	<u>Sample Answer</u>
CHARGE:	A B ● D
(A) release	
(B) belittle	
(C) accuse	
(D) conspire	

Part II—Sentence Completion

Each question in Part II is made up of a sentence with one blank. Each blank indicates that a word or phrase is missing. The sentence is followed by four answer choices. Select the word or phrase that will best complete the meaning of the sentence as a whole.

SAMPLE QUESTIONS:	<u>Sample Answer</u>
It rained so much that the streets were _____.	● B C D
(A) flooded	
(B) arid	
(C) paved	
(D) crowded	
The house was so dirty that it took _____.	A B C ●
(A) less than 10 min to wash it	
(B) four months to demolish it	
(C) over a week to walk across it	
(D) two days to clean it	

Part I—Synonyms

Directions:

Select the word that is most nearly the same in meaning as the word in capital letters.

1. ACME:

   (A) peak   (B) final   (C) bottom   (D) foot

2. AMASS:

   (A) dissipate   (B) accrue   (C) vanish   (D) dissolve

3. CAPACIOUS:

   (A) small   (B) crowded   (C) vast   (D) cramped

4. EXTOL:

   (A) criticize   (B) condemn   (C) attack   (D) laud

5. HECKLE:

   (A) taunt   (B) cheer   (C) encourage   (D) inspire

6. INTRACTABLE:

   (A) obedient   (B) complex   (C) manageable   (D) compliant

7. PERFUNCTORY:

   (A) careful   (B) thorough   (C) hasty   (D) rigorous

8. ROBUST:

   (A) weak   (B) frail   (C) fragile   (D) sturdy

9. SLAVISH:

   (A) independent   (B) original   (C) assertive   (D) subservient

10. SUCCINCT:

(A) lengthy (B) verbose (C) concise (D) long

11. VOUCH:

(A) oppose (B) certify (C) object (D) debunk

12. ACQUIESCE:

(A) permit (B) forbid (C) disallow (D) pause

13. AMBIGUOUS:

(A) cryptic (B) clear (C) obvious (D) plain

14. ARDENT:

(A) passive (B) weak (C) passionate (D) tepid

15. BEQUEATH:

(A) steal (B) reimburse (C) entrust (D) recoup

16. IMPENDING:

(A) remote (B) impossible (C) distant (D) imminent

17. INTREPID:

(A) coward (B) fearful (C) shy (D) confident

18. PRATTLE:

(A) silent (B) chatter (C) ignore (D) miss

19. DIAPHANOUS:

(A) opaque (B) sheer (C) thick (D) armored

20. DIDACTIC:

(A) educational (B) scandalous (C) insignificant (D) futile

Part II—Sentence Completion

Directions:

Select the word that best completes the sentence.

21. There is no other way to _____ the country's crisis but ask help from foreign nations.

    (A) ameliorate   (B) deteriorate   (C) worsen   (D) aggravate

22. It is said that if you _____ happiness to others, you will get much more in return.

    (A) take   (B) ask   (C) steal   (D) bestow

23. Any student who is seen to violate the rules will be _____.

    (A) commended   (B) castigated   (C) rewarded   (D) recognized

24. One needs to have a _____ spirit to appear in the presence of the fierce CEO.

    (A) shy   (B) melancholic   (C) dauntless   (D) timid

25. Caroline _____ when confronted by the committee for the missing funds.

    (A) laughed   (B) smiled   (C) digressed   (D) submitted

26. The manager left _____ remarks to lighten the mood after announcing a company-wide retrenchment.

    (A) facetious   (B) hurtful   (C) serious   (D) intelligent

27. There was no _____ that they adore each other since they talk about each other so much.

    (A) thinking   (B) gainsaying   (C) guessing   (D) confirming

28. The reasons of their fights are _____ to make them separate.

    (A) huge   (B) serious   (C) critical   (D) negligible

29. Being the popular kid at school, Dustin _____ dresses in designer and treats his group to lavish lunch.

    (A) ostentatiously   (B) humbly   (C) wisely   (D) frugally

30. I was left _____ by his grand gesture this morning after our big fight last night.

(A) perplexed   (B) jubilant   (C) grateful   (D) charismatic

31. It is always wise to do everything with _____ so you do not _____ in the end.

(A) haste ... fail   (B) impulsiveness ... miss   (C) prudence ... regret   (D) carelessness ... win

32. After what he had done to cause the failure of this project, there is no _____ to his _____.

(A) mentioning ... participation   (B) recognition ... decision   (C) reward ... contribution

(D) reconciliation ... betrayal

33. Take time to _____ so you can decide on this matter with _____ care.

(A) fantasize ... minute   (B) ruminate ... utmost   (C) binge ... decent   (D) study ... negligible

34. Her ex-fiancé couldn't _____ with her _____ demands since she changes her mind in a heartbeat.

(A) tolerate ... thoughtful   (B) keep up ... whimsical   (C) fulfill ... humble   (D) understand ... shy

35. Pride was what _____ their wonderful _____ so they each started their own companies after the split.

(A) initiated ... relationship   (B) started ... kinship   (C) created ... bond   (D) sundered ... partnership

36. After careful deliberation, both parties _____ agreed to share the project and work _____.

(A) doubtfully ... as one   (B) furiously ... separately   (C) amicably ... together

(D) sadly ... competitively

37. He mastered the art of _____ and have _____ clients to invest in him only to fall into a scam after releasing the fund to him.

(A) artifice ... deceived   (B) business ... convinced   (C) persuasion ... influenced

(D) communication ... invited

38. Unknowingly, his business partner and his fiancée are _____ to defame him _____ his back.

(A) announcing ... below   (B) studying ... within   (C) conniving ... behind   (D) protesting ... on

39. There is only a way in and no way to _____ so think before you _____ into a lifelong commitment.

(A) linger ... skip   (B) egress ... jump   (C) enjoy ... hop   (D) standout ... swim

40. She fell for his _____ talk despite his _____ behavior when around friends.

(A) tough ... serious   (B) sweet ... impish   (C) incomprehensible ... smart   (D) petty ... intelligent

End of section.

If you have any time left, go over the questions in this section only.

Do not start the next section.

You have 35 minutes to answer the 37 questions in the Quantitative Reasoning Section.

Each question is followed by four suggested answers. Read each question and then decide which one of the four suggested answers is best.

Find the row of spaces on your document that has the same number as the question. In this row, mark the space having the same letter as the answer you have chosen. You may write in your test booklet.

EXAMPLE 1:   Sample Answer

What is the value of the expression $(4 + 6) \div 2$?   A   B   ●   D

(A) 2
(B) 4
(C) 5
(D) 7

The correct answer is 5, so circle C is darkened.

EXAMPLE 2:

A square has an area of 25 cm². What is the length of one of its   A   ●   C   D
side?

(A) 1 cm
(B) 5 cm
(C) 10 cm
(D) 25 cm

The correct answer is 5 cm, so circle B is darkened.

Part I—Word Problems (20 QS)

Each question in Part I is consisting of a word problem followed by four answer choices. Look at the four answer choices given and select the best answer.

1. If g is a positive integer and $(x + 8)^2 = x^2 + gx + 64$, then g is equal to what value?

    (A) 8   (B) 4   (C) 16   (D) 12

2. JD is three years older than Veronica and five years younger than Chan. If Veronica is 17 years old, how old is Chan?

    (A) 22 years old   (B) 23 years old   (C) 24 years old   (D) 25 years old

3. W is a whole number divisible by 5. W is also divisible by 4. Which of the following is NOT a possible value for W?

    (A) 20   (B) 30   (C) 40   (D) 60

4. Felix is going on a trip to the zoo. He drove an average speed of 65 miles per hour, and it took him one-and-a-half hours to get from his house to the zoo. How far is the zoo from his house?

    (A) 97.5 miles   (B) 98 miles   (C) 95.5 miles   (D) 96 miles

5. If $x^2 + y^2 = 49$ and $2xy = 14$, what is the value of $(x - y)^2$?

    (A) 14   (B) 35   (C) 17   (D) 7

6. The second angle of a triangle is twice the first angle. The third angle is 20° less than the first. Find the three angles.

    (A) 50°, 100°, 30°   (B) 55°, 110°, 15°   (C) 40°, 80°, 60°   (D) 45°, 90°, 45°

7. Find the dimensions of a rectangle if the perimeter is 150 cm and the length is 15 cm greater than the width.

    (A) 40 cm and 30 cm   (B) 45 m and 30 m   (C) 40 m and 30 m   (D) 45 cm and 30 cm

8. Will scored 98, 88, and 96 on his first three math tests. He still has one test to finish. What score does he need on his fourth test to bring his average up to a 95?

    (A) 93   (B) 98   (C) 95   (D) 90

9. If a, b, and c are consecutive odd integers, then what is the product of a and c if b is 23?

    (A) 252   (B) 525   (C) 452   (D) 352

10. Jill wants to bake chocolate chip cookies. The recipe for the cookies uses 1 cup of flour for 12 cookies. How much flour will you need to make 21 cookies?

(A) $1\frac{1}{2}$ (B) $1\frac{1}{4}$ (C) $1\frac{3}{4}$ (D) $1\frac{1}{3}$

11. The price of a pair of trousers is $70. If you buy three pairs, you will get 10% discount. How much do you have to pay if you buy six pairs?

(A) $336   (B) $363   (C) $360   (D) $330

12. Calypso wants to put new carpet in her rectangular bedroom, which is 11 ft long and 9 ft wide. If carpet costs $6 per square foot, how much will she spend on the carpet? (Assuming that she wants to cover the whole bedroom floor.)

(A) $590   (B) $592   (C) $595   (D) $594

13. Which of the following is NOT the product of two even numbers?

(A) 168   (B) 211   (C) 288   (D) 192

14. The price of a math book is $50, but you have only $35 with you. How much money do you need to borrow from a friend so that you can buy the book?

(A) $15   (B) $20   (C) $25   (D) $10

15. The sum of five times a number and 8 is 48. Find the number.

(A) 6   (B) 7   (C) 8   (D) 9

16. A two-digit number is seven times the sum of its digits. The number formed by reversing the digits is 18 less than the given number. Find the given number.

(A) 24   (B) 32   (C) 23   (D) 42

17. Leslie is 28 years older than Xavier. In six years, Leslie will be three times as old as Xavier. How old is Leslie now?

(A) 30 years old   (B) 36 years old   (C) 32 years old   (D) 34 years old

18. Emerald and her mom arrived at the doctor's office at 10:30 a.m. They see the doctor at 11:10 a.m. How long was their wait?

(A) 35 min   (B) 30 min   (C) 45 min   (D) 40 min

19. A train moves at a speed of 45 km/hr. How far will it travel in 30 min?

(A) 22.5 km   (B) 25.2 km   (C) 20.5 km   (D) 23.2 km

20. What is the product of 5.7 and 100?

(A) 570   (B) 57.0   (C) 5.70   (D) 0.570

Part II—Quantitative Comparison (17 QS)

All questions in Part II are quantitative comparisons between the quantities shown in Column A and Column B. Using the information given in each question, compare the quantity in Column A to the quantity in Column B, and choose one of these four answer choices:

(A) the quantity in Column A is greater

(B) the quantity in Column B is greater

(C) the two quantities are equal

(D) the relationship cannot be determined from the information given

1. The volume of a solid cube is 64 cm^3.

Column A	Column B
The side of the cube	5

2.

Column A	Column B
$10 - 28 \div 2 \times 4 + 7$	32

3.

Column A	Column B
Subtract 15 from 26	Subtract 11 from 24

4.

Column A	Column B
The even number after 37	The odd number before 40

5. A rectangle has sides measuring 3 cm and 7 cm.

Column A	Column B
Area of the rectangle	Perimeter of the rectangle

6.

Column A	Column B
$(1/7) + (1/14)$	$(1/4) + (3/8)$

7.

Column A	Column B
$3(x + 9)$	$3x + 27$

8.

Column A	Column B
Number of tens in 59	Number of hundreds in 523

9.

Column A	Column B
Distance around the triangle if each side has length of 10	Distance around the square if each side has length 7.5

10.

Column A	Column B
$0 \times 9 \times 7$	$5 \times 10 \times 0$

11. A box contains four hats, five shirts, and six handkerchiefs. Two items are removed from the box.

Column A	Column B
The probability that both items are hats	The probability that one item is a handkerchief and the other is a shirt

12. Mr. Leo sells fruit in the market. Apple costs $1.4 per kilogram and grape costs $2.3 per kilogram.

Column A	Column B
The total cost of 7 kg of apples	The total cost of 4 kg of grapes

13. In a class of 40 students, 65% of the students study Spanish.

Column A	Column B
The number of students who study Spanish	26

14. $(x + 5)(y - 3) = 0$

Column A	Column B
x	y

15. The sum of three consecutive whole numbers is 288.

Column A	Column B
The smallest of the three numbers	96

16. Red has planted vegetable seeds in his rectangular garden with an area of 169 sq. ft. To prevent people from walking on the garden, he will enclose the perimeter of the entire garden with rope.

Column A	Column B
The number of feet of rope he needs	51

17.

Column A	Column B
$6x + 2y$	$4x - 7y$

End of section.

If you have any time left, go over the questions in this section only.

Do not start the next section.

You have 35 minutes to answer the 36 questions in the Reading Comprehension and Vocabulary section.

Directions:

This section contains six short reading passages. Each passage is followed by six questions based on its content. Answer the questions following each passage on the basis of what is stated or implied in that passage. You may write in your test booklet.

Questions 1–6

The struggle to elect a House speaker this week was emblematic of a recent trend in American politics in which small groups have obstructed, delayed, or defeated the will of the people.

The most powerful people on Capitol Hill this week weren't party leaders and Hill veterans. It wasn't Rep. Kevin McCarthy, who suffered through vote after failed vote to become speaker of the House, a role he has awaited for decades. It wasn't even the Republican caucus, which as the incoming ruling party overwhelmingly cast their ballots for McCarthy to be leader of the House and second in line to the presidency.

All the power this week was held by a small group of rogue Republicans, many of whom are best known for their denial of the 2020 election or legal troubles—if they are known to the public at large at all. By continually refusing McCarthy the speakership—and without another GOP candidate with broad support to take his place— the group left the House unsettled, ungoverned and unable to do the basic work of democracy and legislating.

On its face, it sounds like a denial of the underlying underline{tenets} of democracy, where phrases like "the will of the people" and "majority rule" are considered the fairest way to resolve differences.

But in reality, the impasse on the House floor reflected the new state of American politics, one in which the minority rules.

Donald Trump won the presidency in 2016 even while losing the national popular vote. In the Senate—where the very makeup of the chamber gives disproportionate power to smaller states, which get the same number of senators as large states—increasingly commonplace threats of filibusters have meant that a minority can (and often has) held up legislation that had majority support. And because Democrats hold such a narrow majority in the chamber, a single Democrat has sometimes exercised outsized influence on legislation, aware his or her vote was critical to final passage.

1. What is the main topic of the passage?

   (A) how small groups have affected the election of a House speaker

   (B) Rep. Kevin McCarthy was the most powerful person on Capitol Hills

   (C) the Republicans overwhelmingly cast their ballots for McCarthy

   (D) McCarthy's triumphant election as the House speaker

2. How have the small group of rogue Republicans affected the election of a House speaker according to the passage?

   (A) they have obstructed, delayed, or defeated the will of the majority

   (B) they did not cast a vote

   (C) they voted for the opposing party

   (D) they did not appear on House floor

3. What does the phrase "the will of the people" mean?

   (A) general will   (B) complaints of the people   (C) minority rules   (D) people's protest

4. According to the passage, what has become the new state of American politics?

   (A) majority rules   (B) minority rules   (C) the will of the people will prevail   (D) democracy for all

5. What does the underlined word in line 2 mean?

   (A) absence   (B) lack of   (C) indicative   (D) truth

6. What does the underlined word in line 25 mean?

   (A) sport   (B) tens   (C) assignments   (D) principle

Questions 7–12

The Biden administration appears eager to switch to an annual COVID-19 booster strategy, but the coronavirus and its many variants pose difficulties.

When President Joe Biden rolled up his sleeve to get the updated COVID-19 booster in October, he pledged that the majority of Americans would only need one coronavirus shot a year.

"For most Americans, one COVID shot each year will be all they need," Biden said at the White House. "And if you get it, you'll be protected. And if you don't, you're putting yourself and other people at unnecessary risk."

He has also spread the idea on Twitter, saying: "Our nation's experts say that most folks will only need one updated COVID vaccine to stay protected all year long. One shot, once a year. Just like flu."

Several of Biden's top health officials have echoed the message.

"It is becoming increasingly clear that, looking forward with the COVID-19 pandemic, in the absence of a dramatically different variant, we likely are moving toward a path with a vaccination cadence similar to that of the annual influenza vaccine, with annual updated COVID-19 shots matched to the currently circulating strains for most of the population," leading infectious disease expert Anthony Fauci said in September.

But more than three months after the Biden administration first floated the idea of an annual COVID-19 booster shot, no official policy has been announced as questions and hurdles remain.

For one, the ever-changing pool of COVID-19 variants makes it difficult to formulate a shot that exactly matches what is circulating—a similar challenge faced by the flu vaccine every season. The updated bivalent shots were designed to take on omicron subvariants BA.4 and BA.5 as well as the original coronavirus strain. Since the shots rolled out at the end of August, the variant scene has—not surprisingly—changed.

7. What is the main topic of the passage?

   (A) the lack of cooperation by the majority to comply with the annual COVID-19 booster

   (B) the lack of budget to switch to an annual COVID-19 booster

   (C) the plan to switch to an annual COVID-19 booster but is faced by difficulties due to the many variants of the coronavirus

   (D) debate on how many shots annually a person should have to stay protected from the virus

8. How did Anthony Fauci envision the COVID-19 booster in September according to the passage?

   (A) in the absence of a dramatically different variant of the coronavirus, we'll be able to switch to an annual COVID-19 booster like that of the annual influenza vaccine

   (B) it will be challenging to formulate an annual COVID-19 booster that will match the circulating variant unlike the influenza vaccine

   (C) we will move forward to a quarterly COVID-19 vaccination due to the change of variant as the seasons change

   (D) there is no need to do an annual COVID-19 booster like that of the influenza vaccine

9. What is the current dilemma of implementing the annual COVID-19 booster?

   (A) the expensive material and production cost of the vaccine

   (B) the ever-changing pool of COVID-19 variants

   (C) the health risk the vaccine poses

   (D) the short shelf-life of the vaccine

10. How many shots in a year does a person need according to the proposed annual COVID-19 booster?

    (A) 2   (B) 3   (C) 1   (D) 0

11. What does the underlined word in line 21 mean?

    (A) disputed   (B) argued   (C) debunked   (D) reverberated

12. What does the underlined word in line 35 mean?

    (A) obstacle   (B) peak   (C) epiphany   (D) climax

Questions 13–18

The fertile soil may be a massive, overlooked source of stored carbon.

Indigenous people in the Amazon may have been deliberately creating fertile soil for farming for thousands of years.

At archaeological sites across the Amazon River basin, mysterious patches of unusually fertile soil dot the landscape. Scientists have long debated the origin of this "dark earth," which is darker in color than surrounding soils and richer in carbon.

Now, researchers have shown that indigenous Kuikuro people in southeastern Brazil intentionally create similar soil around their villages. The finding, presented December 16 at the American Geophysical Union meeting, adds evidence to the idea that long-ago Amazonians deliberately manufactured such soil too.

The fact that Kuikuro people make dark earth today is a "pretty strong argument" that people were also making it in the past, says Paul Baker, a geochemist at Duke University who was not involved in the research.

In doing so, these early inhabitants may have inadvertently stored massive quantities of carbon in the soil, says study presenter Taylor Perron, an earth scientist at MIT. The technique, he says, could provide a blueprint for developing methods of sustainably locking atmospheric carbon in tropical soils, helping fight climate change.

The Western world has long viewed the Amazon as a vast wilderness that was relatively untouched before Europeans showed up. At the center of this argument is the idea that the Amazon's soil, which is poor in nutrients like other tropical soils, precluded its inhabitants from developing agriculture at a scale required to support complex societies.

But a slew of archeological finds in recent decades—including the discovery of ancient urban centers in Amazonian areas of modern-day Bolivia—has revealed that people were actively shaping the Amazon for thousands of years before the arrival of Europeans (SN: 5/25/22).

13. What is the main topic of the passage?

(A) agriculture is not the main source of livelihood in the Amazon

(B) the soil in the amazon is poor in nutrients and not ideal for farming

(C) further proof that the Amazon was a vast wilderness before the arrival of Europeans

(D) new evidence that the indigenous people may have been actively shaping the Amazon by deliberately creating fertile soil

14. What recent evidence did the researchers find to prove that people in the amazon were deliberately creating "dark earth"?

(A) the indigenous Kuikuro people in southeastern Brazil intentionally create similar soil around their villages

(B) the researchers attempted to create "dark earth"

(C) the researchers were able to talk to the elders of the indigenous people

(D) a writing of the steps how the indigenous people created dark earth was found

15. What does "dark earth" mean according to the passage?

(A) black mud   (B) fertile soil   (C) rocky topsoil   (D) dark-colored clay

16. According to the research about the "dark earth," what was the purpose of this soil?

(A) for beautification   (B) for building   (C) for farming   (D) for fire

17. What is the meaning of the underlined word in line 12?

(A) nomad who travels from one place to another

(B) foreign from another origin

(C) inhabiting or existing in a land from the earliest times or from before the arrival of colonists

(D) immigrant who settled to a new place

18. What is the meaning of the underlined word in line 37?

(A) prohibited   (B) permitted   (C) allowed   (D) encouraged

Questions 19–24

Scientists have pinpointed bacteria that make cheese taste fruity, musty, or oniony.

Cheese making has been around for thousands of years, and there are now more than 1,000 varieties of cheese worldwide. But what exactly makes some cheeses like Parmesan taste fruity and others, such as Brie and Camembert, taste musty has remained a bit of a mystery. Now, scientists have <u>pinned down</u> the specific types of bacteria that produce these flavor compounds.

The findings, described November 10 in Microbiology Spectrum, could help cheese makers more precisely <u>tweak</u> cheese flavor profiles to better match consumer preferences, say food microbiologist Morio Ishikawa and colleagues.

A cheese's flavor depends on more than the type of milk and starter bacteria used to make the fermented dairy delight. A constellation of organisms that move in during the cheese-ripening process also contributes to the flavor (SN: 5/14/16).

Ishikawa, of the Tokyo University of Agriculture, likens these nonstarter bacteria to an orchestra. "We can perceive the tones played by the orchestra of cheese as a harmony, but we do not know what instruments each of them is responsible for."

Previous research by Ishikawa and colleagues used genetic analysis, gas chromatography and mass spectrometry to link specific flavor molecules with specific types of bacteria on surface mold–ripened cheeses made from pasteurized and raw cow milk in Japan and France.

In the new study, to show that each bacterial suspect was responsible for producing the flavor compound it had been linked to, the team unleashed each type of microbe onto its own unripe cheese sample. The researchers then observed how flavor compounds in the cheese changed over 21 days.

19. What is the main topic of the passage?

    (A) three main cheese flavors are fruity, musty, and oniony

    (B) there are more than 1,000 varieties of cheese worldwide

    (C) that cheese making has been around for thousands of years

    (D) how scientist have pinpointed bacteria that make each cheese flavor which will benefit cheese makers in precisely tweaking cheese flavor profiles

20. How will this discovery affect the cheese industry according to the passage?

    (A) this will give rise to more unique cheese flavors

    (B) this finding could help cheese makers more precisely tweak cheese flavor to better match consumer preferences

    (C) the cheese makers will go bankrupt since everyone discovered the secret to making each flavor

    (D) cheese making will stop being an art form

21. How many days did the researchers spend observing how flavor compounds in the cheese changed?

    (A) a little less than 21 days   (B) a day after 21   (C) over 21 days   (D) 20 days

22. Where does the cheese's flavor depend on?

    (A) the flavor depends on a harmony of organisms more than the type of milk and starter bacteria used to make the cheese   (B) solely the type of milk   (C) environment   (D) temperature

23. What does the underlined compound word in line 9 mean?

    (A) to put a pin and stick on a board   (B) to hold someone down by pushing

    (C) to understand or describe something exactly   (D) to let go

24. What does the underlined word in line 13 mean?

    (A) to twist and break   (B) to alter and make unrecognizable

    (C) to replace entirely   (D) change something slightly with the purpose of making it correct

Questions 25–30

Star-aligned ritual centers along Mexico's Gulf Coast date to as early as 3,100 years ago.

Olmec and Maya people living along Mexico's Gulf Coast as early as 3,100 years ago built star-aligned ceremonial centers to track important days of a 260-day calendar, a new study finds.

The oldest written evidence of this calendar, found on painted plaster mural fragments from a Maya site in Guatemala, dates to between 300 and 200 B.C., nearly a millennium later (SN: 4/13/22). But researchers have long suspected that a 260-day calendar developed hundreds of years earlier among Gulf Coast Olmec groups.

Now, an airborne laser-mapping technique called light detection and ranging, or lidar, has revealed astronomical orientations of 415 ceremonial complexes dating to between about 1100 B.C. and A.D. 250, say archaeologist Ivan Šprajc and colleagues. Most ritual centers were aligned on an east-to-west axis, corresponding to sunrises or other <u>celestial</u> events on specific days of a 260-day year, the scientists report January 6 in Science Advances.

The finding points to the earliest evidence in the Americas of a formal calendar system that combined astronomical knowledge with earthly constructions. This system used celestial events to identify important dates during a 260-day portion of a full year.

"The 260-day cycle <u>materialized</u> in Mesoamerica's earliest known monumental complexes [and was used] for scheduling seasonal, subsistence-related ceremonies," says Šprajc, of the Research Center of the Slovenian Academy of Sciences and Arts in Ljubljana. "We cannot be certain exactly when and where it was invented."

Some of the oldest ceremonial centers identified by lidar clearly belong to the Olmec culture, but others are hard to classify, says archaeologist Stephen Houston of Brown University in Providence, R.I., who did not participate in the new study.

25. What is the main topic of the passage?

(A) how long ago the rituals were along Mexico's Gulf Coast

(B) the oldest known formal calendar that uses both astronomical knowledge and earth structures

(C) how the Maya charted the stars and named constellations

(D) how the calendar evolved from 260 days to 365 days

26. How many days was the calendar of the Olmec and Maya people living along Mexico's Gulf Coast?

(A) $260\frac{1}{4}$-day cycle   (B) 365-day cycle   (C) 260-day cycle   (D) 366-day cycle

27. According to the passage, what was the 260-day calendar used for in Mesoamerica?

(A) used for picking the best date to hold a wedding   (B) used for birthdays

(C) used for scheduling seasonal, subsistence-related ceremonies   (D) used to celebrate Christmas

28. What was the latest technique used to reveal the star-aligned ritual centers?

(A) airborne laser-mapping technique called light detection and ranging, or lidar

(B) painted plaster mural fragments   (C) telescope   (D) microscope

29. What does the underlined word in line 22 mean?

(A) pertaining to or relating to the sky   (B) with unearthly beauty

(C) possessing godly power   (D) flawless being

30. What does the underlined word in line 31 mean?

(A) become solid   (B) emerged   (C) vanished   (D) forgotten

Questions 31–36

Like tree rings, layers of water pockets also preserve a record of an icicle's growth.

Tiny drops of dirty water, often mistaken for air bubbles, tell the tale of rippling icicle growth.

Icicles made of pure water are smooth. But salt or other impurities make icicles develop ripples as they hang from branches, bridges, and power lines (SN: 11/24/13). Impurities are also responsible for the hazy appearance of icicles that has typically been attributed to air bubbles. Those bubbles are actually minute dollops of contaminated water, researchers report in the November *Physical Review E*.

While examining 3-millimeter-thick cross sections of icicles grown in the lab, University of Toronto physicists Stephen Morris and John Ladan uncovered pockets of impure, liquid water surrounded by relatively pure ice (SN: 8/13/10). "It turns out that there are very few air bubbles in an icicle," Morris says. He calls the water pockets "inclusions" to distinguish them from air bubbles.

What's more, "the inclusions record the history of the growth of the ripples. It's like the rings in a tree," Morris says. Inclusions form in layers near the surface of an icicle, with older layers covered by younger ones as an icicle grows. "You can deduce something about the history of the growth by looking at the pattern of inclusions."

To track icicle formation, the researchers mixed fluorescent dye into water in place of other types of impurities and used the water to grow icicles in the lab. The dye ended up concentrating at higher levels in liquid inclusions in the icicles, just as any other contaminant would. It also glowed brightly under ultraviolet light, which made the inclusion layers easier to see.

31. What is the main topic of passage?

(A) how cold should the temperature be to form icicles

(B) proof that tiny bubbles in icicles are filled with air

(C) what is inside the tiny bubbles that make icicles hazy

(D) types of icicles and how they are formed

32. According to the passage, what are the tiny bubbles in hazy icicles filled with?

(A) contaminated water   (B) carbon   (C) oxygen   (D) lead

33. How was the study to identify what is inside the tiny bubbles in icicles conducted?

(A) researchers went to Antarctica to get samples of icicles

(B) scientists gathered slabs of ice from Iceland

(C) researchers studied icicles formed in caves during winter

(D) researchers grew icicles in the lab and mixed fluorescent dye into water in place of other types of impurities

34. After reading the passage, do all icicles appear hazy? Why?

(A) Yes, because of contaminants and other impurities.

(B) No, icicles made of pure water are smooth, but salt or other impurities make icicles develop ripples which make them hazy.

(C) Maybe, there is no telling for sure.

(D) Maybe, it depends on what season of the year the icicles are formed.

35. What does the underlined word in line 11 mean?

(A) 60 s   (B) notes from a meeting   (C) extremely small   (D) large

36. What does the underlined word in line 28 mean?

(A) wonder   (B) falsify   (C) rebuke   (D) conclude

End of section.

If you have any time left, go over the questions in this section only.

Do not start the next section.

You have 40 minutes to answer the 47 questions in the Mathematics Achievement Section.

Each question is followed by four suggested answers. Read each question and then decide which one of the four suggested answers is best.

Find the row of spaces on your document that has the same number as the question. In this row, mark the space having the same letter as the answer you have chosen. You may write in your test booklet.

SAMPLE QUESTION: Sample Answer

Which of the numbers below is not factor of 364?   A ● C D

(A) 13
(B) 20
(C) 26
(D) 91

The correct answer is 20, so circle B is darkened.

---

1. An octagon has a perimeter of 128 in. Find the length of one side.

    (A) 15 (B) 16 (C) 17 (D) 18

2. Eleonor is conducting a survey regarding gender identity and its effect on the society. She is wants to interview a total of 150 participants. The ratio of male to female participants will be 3:2. How many female participants she needs to interview?

    (A) 30 (B) 60 (C) 90 (D) 75

3. What is the sum of all the interior angles of a decagon (a polygon with 10 sides)?

    (A) 1260 (B) 1620 (C) 1400 (D) 1440

    For questions 4–5, please refer to the table below.

    Teacher Mari recorded her students' grades in the group activity they completed earlier in the table below.

Groups	Grades
A	92
B	95
C	93
D	92
E	94

4. What is the average grade the class got?

(A) 93.2   (B) 94.2   (C) 93.8   (D) 92.7

5. What is the median of the grade/data collected?

(A) 92   (B) 93   (C) 94   (D) 95

6. Multiply $x^5 \cdot x^2$

(A) x^{10} (B) x^5 (C) x^2 (D) x^7

7. What is three-fourths of one-third?

(A) $\dfrac{2}{5}$ (B) $\dfrac{1}{4}$ (C) $\dfrac{1}{3}$ (D) $\dfrac{3}{7}$

8. Simplify the following expression: $(4x^7y^3)(11x^2y^9)$

(A) $44x^{14}y^{27}$ (B) $44x^9y^{12}$ (C) $44x^5y^7$ (D) $44x^9y^{27}$

9. Brian has three siblings. When his family ordered pizza, each of the four children is given $\dfrac{1}{4}$ of the pizza. Brian does not feel well so he only finishes $\dfrac{1}{3}$ of his pizza. If the original pizza consisted of 12 slices of pizza, how many slices did Brian eat?

(A) 2   (B) 4   (C) 3   (D) 1

10. Solve the following equation for g when is l equal to 8

$$\frac{g^3 - 75}{5} = l + 2$$

(A) 3   (B) 4   (C) 5   (D) 6

11. Mara works in a flower shop. She has a monthly salary of $100 and a commission of $3.25 for each bouquet she sells. How much money will she make this month if she sells 15 bouquets of flowers?

(A) $148.75   (B) $147.85   (C) $148.50   (D) $147.75

12. Consider the following system: $x - y = 7$ and $2x + y = 8$. What is the sum of x and y?

(A) 5   (B) 7   (C) –4   (D) 3

13. The mean of 17 test scores is 83. When the 18th student takes the test, the mean goes down by two points. Give the 18th score.

(A) 74   (B) 47   (C) 65   (D) 81

14. If the two triangles are similar, then what is the ratio of their perimeter?

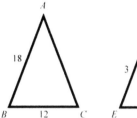

(A) 3:1   (B) 5:2   (C) 6:1   (D) 4:3

15. Define the function: $k(x) = | x^4 - x^2 |$, when $k(5)$

(A) 600   (B) 700   (C) 500   (D) 800

16. How many numbers between 1 and 40, inclusive, are both prime and a multiple of 4?

(A) 4   (B) 1   (C) 2   (D) 0

17. JM bought a variety pack of snacks. It contains five bags of Lays, two bags of Cheetos, three bags of Doritos, and three bags of Nova. The Lays make up what percentage of the variety pack?

(A) 38.46%   (B) 15.38%   (C) 23.07%   (D) 40%

18. Find the x-intercept of a line with a slope of 4 and a point of (4,4).

(A) 3   (B) 4   (C) 2   (D) 0

19. Nini runs 3 miles every day and walks 5 miles every day. When Nini has completed a total of 40 miles, how many miles will she have walked?

(A) 15 miles   (B) 20 miles   (C) 25 miles   (D) 30 miles

20. Simplify: $459.84 \div 35.42$

(A) 12.98   (B) 12.89   (C) 12.99   (D) 12.88

21. Simplify: $24 - 6^2 \div (9 + 3)$

(A) 21   (B) –1   (C) 1.66   (D) 23

22. Find the volume of a cone with a base diameter of 4 and a height of 12.

(A) 12π (B) 10π (C) 16π (D) 14π

23. Factor the number 429 to all of its prime factors.

(A) 3, 11, 13   (B) 2, 3, 26   (C) 2, 11, 13   (D) 2, 3, 13

24. In a rectangle, the width is 9 ft long and the length is 12 ft long. If a diagonal is drawn through the rectangle, from one corner to the other, how many feet long is that diagonal?

    (A) 12 ft   (B) 14 ft   (C) 15 ft   (D) 13 ft

25. Clara has a very small, square-shaped dorm room. She tells you that it is only 289 sq. ft. Assuming this is true, what is the perimeter of her room?

    (A) 73 ft   (B) 60 ft   (C) 70 ft   (D) 68 ft

26. What is the greatest common factor of 12, 30, and 48?

    (A) 3   (B) 6   (C) 12   (D) 4

27. What is the least common multiple of 8 and 20?

    (A) 40   (B) 20   (C) 80   (D) 60

28. Evaluate: $\dfrac{30}{15^0 - 10^0}$

    (A) 0   (B) 1   (C) 6   (D) the expression is undefined

29. Find the roots of $x^2 - 4x - 21$

    (A) $x = -3, x = 7$ (B) $x = 3, x = -7$ (C) $x = 3, x = -3$ (D) $x = -7, x = 7$

30. Simplify: $2x^2y - 5xy^2 + 3xy - 4xy^2 + x^2y$

    (A) $3x^2y - 9x^2y + 3xy^2$ (B) $3xy^2 - 9x^2y + 3xy$ (C) $3x^2y - 9xy^2 + 3xy$ (D) $3x^2y^2 - 9xy^2 + 3xy$

31. Larry makes a weekly salary of $1,700 at his sales-based job. His weekly quota of sales is $15,000, with a 10% commission on all sales beyond the weekly quota. What will his income be for a week in which he makes a total sale of $21,000?

    (A) $1,300   (B) $1,700   (C) $2,000   (D) $2,300

    Use the chart below for questions 32–34.

Color	Number of balls
Red	12
Yellow	9
Blue	9
Green	10

32. If these are the colors of the balls inside the box, what would be the probability of getting two consecutive blue balls?

    (A) $\dfrac{9}{40}$ (B) $\dfrac{3}{65}$ (C) $\dfrac{8}{39}$ (D) $\dfrac{1}{7}$

33. What would be the probability of getting one red then followed by one green?

(A) $\dfrac{5}{52}$ (B) $\dfrac{4}{52}$ (C) $\dfrac{6}{52}$ (D) $\dfrac{7}{52}$

34. What is the probability of getting one yellow?

(A) 25.2%   (B) 23.2%   (C) 24.5%   (D) 22.5%

35. Simplify: $-2x(-2x + 7)$

(A) $4x^2 - 14x$ (B) $4x^2 + 14x$ (C) $-4x^2 - 14x$ (D) $-4x^2 + 14x$

36. Find the value of x in the given sequence: 4, x, 64, 256, 1024

(A) 4   (B) 16   (C) 8   (D) 6

37. Simplify: $\dfrac{\left(x^2 + y^2\right)^2 - \left(x^2 - y^2\right)^2}{x^4 y^4}$

(A) $\dfrac{xy}{x^2 y^z}$ (B) $\dfrac{4}{xy}$ (C) $\dfrac{4}{x^2 y^2}$ (D) $\dfrac{2}{x^2 y^2}$

Use the following data set to answer the questions 38–40.

5, 4, 7, 6, 5, 2, 5, 4, 5, 9, 3

38. What is the mean of the given set?

(A) 4.5   (B) 5   (C) 5.5   (D) 4

39. What is the mode of the set?

(A) 6   (B) 4   (C) 5   (D) 7

40. What is the median of the set?

(A) 6   (B) 4   (C) 5   (D) 7

41. What is the 175% of 60?

(A) 100   (B) 120   (C) 115   (D) 105

42. If a right triangle has a base of 8 and a height of 6, what is the length of the hypotenuse?

(A) 11   (B) 10   (C) 12   (D) $\sqrt{10}$

43. If a pentagon has a perimeter of 95 cm, what is the length of one side of the pentagon?

(A) 16 cm   (B) 19 cm   (C) 18 cm   (D) 17 cm

44. Soo started working on her homework at 6:45 p.m. It took her 1 hr and 57 min to complete it. What time did Soo completed her homework?

(A) 8:40 p.m.   (B) 8:42 p.m.   (C) 8:44 p.m.   (D) 8:45 p.m.

45. Five years ago, Thelma's age was half of the age she will be in eight years. How old is she now?

(A) 15 years old   (B) 16 years old   (C) 17 years old   (D) 18 years old

46. Multiply the following:

$b^4 \times b^3 \times b^2$

(A) b^9 (B) b^{24} (C) b^{12} (D) b^{14}

47. Multiply: $\dfrac{1}{10} \times \dfrac{3}{5} \times \dfrac{5}{2}$

(A) $\dfrac{3}{20}$ (B) $\dfrac{20}{3}$ (C) $\dfrac{3}{10}$ (D) $\dfrac{10}{3}$

End of section.

If you have any time left, go over the questions in this section only.

Do not start the next section.

ANSWER KEY

Verbal Reasoning

1. A	7. C	13. A	19. B	25. C	31. C	37. A
2. B	8. D	14. C	20. A	26. A	32. D	38. C
3. C	9. D	15. C	21. A	27. B	33. B	39. B
4. D	10. C	16. D	22. D	28. D	34. B	40. B
5. A	11. B	17. D	23. B	29. A	35. D	
6. B	12. A	18. B	24. C	30. A	36. C	

Quantitative Reasoning

WORD PROBLEMS		QUANTITATIVE COMPARISONS	
1. C	11. A	1. A	11. B
2. D	12. D	2. B	12. A
3. B	13. B	3. B	13. C
4. A	14. A	4. B	14. D
5. B	15. C	5. A	15. B
6. A	16. D	6. B	16. D
7. D	17. B	7. C	17. D
8. B	18. D	8. C	
9. B	19. A	9. C	
10. C	20. A	10. C	

Part I—Word Problems (20 QS)

1. Answer: **C**

   Expand $(x + 8)^2$ and you will get $(x + 8)(x + 8) = x^2 + 16x + 64$. Hence, $g = 16$ which is C.

2. Answer: **D**

   Since Veronica is 17 years and JD is three years older than her, we just need to add $17 + 3 = 20$ to get JD's age. Chan, on the other hand, is five years older than JD. To get Chan's age, we just need to add 5 to JD's age, $20 + 5 = 25$. Hence, Chan's age is 25 years old which is D.

3. Answer: **B**

   To get the correct answer, we just need to divide the choices by 5 and 4.

   A. $20 \div 5 = 4$, $20 \div 4 = 5$

   B. $30 \div 5 = 6$, $30 \div 5 = 7.5$

   C. $40 \div 5 = 8$, $40 \div 4 = 10$

   D. $60 \div 5 = 12$, $60 \div 4 = 15$

   Out of all the choices, only option B has a decimal when divided by 4, hence the answer is B.

4. Answer: **A**

   To get the distance (d), we need to multiply rate (r) with time (t). $d = rt \implies d = 65$ mph $\times 1.5$ hr. $\implies d = 97.5$ miles, hence the answer is A.

5. Answer: **B**

   Expand the expression $(x^2 - y^2)$ and we will get $(x - y)(x - y) = x^2 - 2xy + y^2$. Rearrange the positions to $x^2 + y^2 - 2xy$. It was given that $x^2 + y^2 = 49$ and $2xy = 14$, we can substitute $49 - 14 = 35$, hence the answer is B.

6. Answer: **A**

   Let x be the first angle, $2x$ the second angle, and $x - 20°$ the third angle. It is given that the sum of the angles in a triangle is $180°$, we can add $x + 2x + x - 20° = 180° \implies 4x - 20° = 180° \implies 4x = 180° + 20° \implies 4x = 200° \implies x = 50°$. We now have the first angle and simply substitute the value of x to get the second and third angles: $2x = 2(50°) = 100°$, $x - 20° = 50° - 20° = 30°$. Hence, the angles measure $50°$, $100°$, and $30°$ which is A.

7. Answer: **D**

   The formula to get the perimeter of a triangle is $P = 2l + 2w$, where l is the length and w is the width. It is given that the length is 15 greater than width, so $l = w + 15$. Substitute, $P = 2l + 2w \implies 150 = 2(w + 15) + 2w \implies 150 = 2w + 30 + 2w \implies 150 = 4w + 30 \implies 4w = 120 \implies w = 30$ cm. To get the length, $l = w + 15 \implies l = 30 + 15 \implies l = 45$ cm. Hence, the dimensions are 45 cm and 30 cm which is D.

8. Answer: **B**

Let x be the score of the fourth test. It is given that average can be calculated by adding all the numbers in a set divided by the total number on that set, $(98 + 88 + 96 + x) \div 4 = 95 \implies (282 + x) \div 4 = 95 \implies 282 + x = 380 \implies x = 98$, hence the answer is B.

9. Answer: **B**

It is given that odd numbers are whole numbers that cannot be divided exactly into pairs. If a, b, and c are consecutive odd integers, we can assume that the numbers are 21, 23, and 25. Multiply 21 and 25 and we will get 525, hence the answer is B.

10. Answer: **C**

Let x be the number of cups of flour needed to bake 21 cookies. The ratio of cups of flour to cookies is 1:12, so $1:12 = x:21$. $\dfrac{1}{12} = \dfrac{x}{21} \implies 12x = 21 \implies x = \dfrac{21}{12} \implies x = 1\dfrac{3}{4}$, hence the answer is C.

11. Answer: **A**

The total price of the six pairs is $\$70 \times 6 = \$420$. To get the discounted price, multiply the total percentage to the total price, $\$420 \times \dfrac{20}{100} = \$84$ and then subtract the result from the total price, $\$420 - \$84 = \$336$. Hence the answer is A.

12. Answer: **D**

To get the area of the bedroom, we need to multiply the length and width, 11 ft $\times$ 9 ft = 99 sq. ft. Multiply it then to the cost of each square feet, 99 sq. ft $\times$ \$6 per sq. ft = \$594, hence the answer is D.

13. Answer: **B**

It is given that the product of two even numbers is even. Among the choices, only option B is not an even number, hence the answer is B.

14. Answer: **A**

To get the amount you need to buy the book, we simply need to subtract the amount you have from the price of the book, $\$50 - \$35 = \$15$. Hence the answer is A.

15. Answer: **C**

Let x be the number. $5x + 8 = 48 \implies 5x = 40 \implies x = 8$. Hence, the answer is C.

16. Answer: **D**

Let xy be the number. The actual value of the number is $10x + y$. With the given condition:

i. $10x + y = 7(x + y) \implies 10x + y = 7x + 7y \implies 10x - 7x = 7y - y \implies 3x = 6y \implies x = 2y$

ii. $10y + x = (10x + y) - 18 \implies$ substitute the value of x with $2y$: $10y + 2y = 10(2y) + y - 18 \implies 12y = 20y + y - 18 \implies 12y = 21y - 18$ $y = 2$

Now that we got the value of y, substitute it to the expression $x = 2y \implies x = 2(2) \implies x = 4$. Hence the answer is 42 which is D.

17. **Answer: B**

	Current Age	Age after Six Years
Xavier	X	$x + 6$
Leslie	$x + 28$	$x + 34$

It is given that in six years, Leslie will be thrice as old as Xavier, $x + 34 = 3(x + 6) \implies x + 34 = 3x + 18 \implies$ $x - 3x = 18 - 34 \implies -2x = -16 \implies x = 8$. We now have the value of x which is Xavier's current age. To get Leslie's current age, add 28 to Xavier's current age, $8 + 28 = 36$. Hence the answer is B.

18. **Answer: D**

A half hour has passed after 10:30 and 10 min has passed after 11:00. Half an hour is 30 min, add then the 10 min = 30 + 10 = 40 min, hence the answer is D.

19. **Answer: A**

To get the distance (d), we need to multiply rate (r) with time (t). $d = rt \implies d = 45$ kmph $\times$ 0.5 hr. $\implies d =$ 22.5 km, hence the answer is A.

20. **Answer: A**

$5.7 \times 100 = 570$, hence the answer is A.

Part II—Quantitative Comparisons (17 QS)

1. **Answer: A**

It is given that the volume of cube is $V = s^3$. To get length of the side, $64 = s^3 \implies \sqrt[3]{64} = \sqrt[3]{s}^3 \implies s = 4$. Five is greater than four, hence the answer is A.

2. **Answer: B**

To evaluate the expression on Column A, apply the PEMDAS rule. There are no parentheses and exponents, so do multiplication and division from left to right: $28 \div 2 \times 4 = 14 \times 4 = 56$, then add and subtract from left to right: $10 - 56 + 7 = -46 + 7 = -36$. A positive number is always greater than a negative number, hence the answer is B.

3. **Answer: B**

Simply $26 - 15 = 11$; $24 - 11 = 13$. Thirteen is greater than 11, hence the answer is B.

4. Answer: **B**

    The even number after 37 is 38 and the odd number before 40 is 39. Thirty-nine is greater than 38, hence the answer is B.

5. Answer: **A**

    It is given that the area of a rectangle is $A = l \times w$ and the perimeter is $P = 2l + 2w$. To get area: 7 cm × 3 cm = 21 cm². To get the perimeter: 2(7 cm) + 2(3 cm) = 14 cm + 6 cm = 20 cm. The area is greater than the perimeter, hence the answer is A.

6. Answer: **B**

    Evaluate the expressions. For Column A, $\frac{1}{7} + \frac{1}{14} = \frac{2+1}{14} = \frac{3}{14} = 0.214$. For Column B, $\frac{1}{4} + \frac{3}{8} = \frac{2+3}{8} = \frac{5}{8} = 0.625$. Column B is greater than Column A, hence the answer is B.

7. Answer: **C**

    If we multiply 3 to the expression $x + 9$, we will get $3x + 27$ which is the same with Column B, hence the answer is C.

8. Answer: **C**

    The tens number in Column A is 5 and the hundreds number in Column B is also 5, hence the answer is C.

9. Answer: **C**

    It is given that the perimeter of a triangle is $P = 3s$ and the perimeter of a square is $P = 4s$. Evaluate the perimeter of the triangle in Column A: $P = 3(10) = 30$. Evaluate the perimeter of the square in column B: $P = 4(7.5) = 30$. Both columns have the same result, hence the answer is C.

10. Answer: **C**

    It is given that any number multiplied by 0 will be 0, hence both columns are the same, so the answer is C.

11. Answer: **B**

    Totally, there are 15 items in the box. For Column A, the probability of getting the first hat is $\frac{4}{15}$ and since one item was already removed, the probability of getting the second hat will be $\frac{3}{14}$. Multiply both expressions, $\frac{4}{15} \cdot \frac{3}{14} = \frac{2}{35} = 5.71\%$. For Column B (assuming you put all the items back on the box), the probability of getting a handkerchief is $\frac{6}{15}$ and since we removed one item, the probability of getting the shirt will be $\frac{5}{14}$. Multiply, $\frac{6}{15} \cdot \frac{5}{14} = \frac{1}{7} = 14.28\%$. Column B is greater than Column A, hence the answer is B.

12. Answer: **A**

Multiply the cost per kilogram of each fruit to get the total cost. For apples, $1.4 per kg × 7 kg = $9.80. For grapes, $2.3 per kg × 4 kg = $9.20. The total cost of the apples is greater than the total cost of the grapes, hence the answer is A.

13. Answer: **C**

To get the number of students studying Spanish, multiply 65% to the total students = $40 \times \frac{65}{100} = 26$. Column A has the same value with Column B, hence the answer is C.

14. Answer: **D**

There's not enough data to get the value of x and y, hence the answer is D.

15. Answer: **B**

Let x be the first number, $x + 1$ be the second number, and $x + 2$ be the third number. $x + x + 1 + x + 2 = 288 \implies 3x + 3 = 288 \implies 3x = 285 \implies x = 95$. The smallest number is 95. Ninety-six is greater than 95, hence the answer is B.

16. Answer: **D**

There's not enough data to get the length of the rope, hence the answer is D.

17. Answer: **D**

There's no value given for x and y, hence the answer is D.

Reading Comprehension and Vocabulary

1. A	7. C	13. D	19. D	25. B	31. C
2. A	8. A	14. A	20. B	26. C	32. A
3. A	9. B	15. B	21. C	27. C	33. D
4. B	10. C	16. C	22. A	28. A	34. B
5. C	11. D	17. C	23. C	29. A	35. C
6. D	12. A	18. A	24. D	30. B	36. D

1. See lines 1–4. The passage talks about how the House floor struggled to elect a new House speaker due to the small groups.

2. See lines 1–4. The passage talks about how the House floor struggled to elect a new House speaker due to the small groups.

3. In political philosophy, the general will is the will of the people as a whole. The term was made famous by 18th-century Genevan philosopher Jean-Jacques Rousseau.

4. See lines 31–33.

5. Emblematic means serving as a symbol of a particular quality or concept. Synonyms are symbolic, indicative, and representative.

6. Tenet is a principle or belief, especially one of the main principles of a religion or philosophy.

7. See lines 1–4. The passage talks about the idea proposed by the Biden administration to switch to an annual COVID-19 booster; however, it is not yet finalized until now due to the changing variants of the virus.

8. See lines 21–30.

9. See lines 36–40.

10. See lines 9–10.

11. To echo means to repeat (someone's words or opinions), typically to express agreement. Synonyms are to repeat, reiterate, and reverberate.

12. A hurdle is an obstacle or difficulty.

13. See lines 3–5.

14. See lines 12–18.

15. See lines 4–11.

16. See lines 3–5.

17. Indigenous means inhabiting or existing in a land from the earliest times or from before the arrival of colonists, native.

18. To preclude means to prevent from happening; make impossible.

19. See lines 1–2, 13–15.

20. See lines 12–15.

21. See lines 30–42.

22. See lines 17–28.

23. To pin down something means to understand or describe something exactly.

24. To tweak means to change something slightly, especially to make it more correct, effective, or suitable.

25. See lines 3–7, 25–28.

26. See line 6.

27. See lines 31–34.

28. See lines 15–17.

29. Celestial means positioned in or relating to the sky, or outer space as observed in astronomy.

30. To materialize is to appear or be present, or to make something happen.

31. See lines 3–5.

32. See lines 3–5.

33. See lines 15–16, 32–34.

34. See lines 6–11.

35. Minute, as used in this sentence, means extremely small in amount.

36. To deduce means to arrive at (a fact or a conclusion) by reasoning; draw as a logical conclusion.

Mathematics Achievement

1. B	11. A	21. A	31. D	41. D
2. B	12. D	22. C	32. B	42. B
3. D	13. B	23. A	33. B	43. B
4. A	14. C	24. C	34. D	44. B
5. B	15. A	25. D	35. A	45. D
6. D	16. D	26. B	36. B	46. A
7. B	17. A	27. A	37. C	47. A
8. B	18. A	28. D	38. B	
9. D	19. C	29. A	39. C	
10. C	20. A	30. C	40. C	

1. Answer: **B**

    It is given that the perimeter of an octagon is $P = 8s$. $128 = 8s \Longrightarrow s = 16$, hence the answer is B.

2. Answer: **B**

    Let x be the participant, $3x$ be the male participants, and $2x$ be the female participants. $3x + 2x = 150 \Longrightarrow 5x = 150 \Longrightarrow x = 30$. To find the female participants, substitute the value of x to $2x = 2(30) = 60$, hence the answer is B.

3. Answer: **D**

    It is given that the sum of the interior angles in a polygon is $t = (n - 2)(180°)$ in which t is the total sum of the angles, and n is equal to the number of sides. A decagon has 10 sides so substitute n with 10: $t = (10 - 2)(180°) = (8)(180°) = 1440°$, hence the answer is D.

4. Answer: **A**

    It is given that average can be calculated by adding all the numbers in a set divided by the total number on that set, so $(92 + 95 + 93 + 92 + 94) \div 5 = 466 \div 5 = 93.2$, hence the answer is A.

5. Answer: **B**

    It is given that median is the middle number in an ordered data set. Arrange the grades: 92, 92, 93, 94, 95. Ninety-three is in the middle, hence the answer is B.

6. Answer: **D**

    When multiplying two expressions with the same base, we apply the rule, $a^x \cdot a^y = a^{x+y}$, in which "a" is the common base and "x" and "y" are the exponents. $x^5 \cdot x^2 = x^{5+2} = x^7$, hence the answer is D.

7. **Answer: B**

   Multiply: $\frac{1}{3} \cdot \frac{3}{4} = \frac{3}{12} = \frac{1}{4}$, hence the answer is B.

8. **Answer: B**

   When multiplying two expressions with the same base, we apply the rule, $a^x \cdot a^y = a^{x+y}$, in which "a" is the common base and "x" and "y" are the exponents. $(4x^7y^3)(11x^2y^9) = (4)(11)\ x^{7+2}\ y^{3+9} = 44x^9y^{12}$, hence the answer is B.

9. **Answer: D**

   Brian's share is $12 \times \frac{1}{4} = 3$ slices. Since he was not feeling well, he only ate $\frac{1}{3}$ of his share: $3 \times \frac{1}{3} = 1$. He only ate one slice, hence the answer is D.

10. **Answer: C**

    Substitute l with 8: $\frac{g^3 - 75}{5} = 8 + 2 \implies \frac{g^3 - 75}{5} = 10 \implies g^3 - 75 = 50 \implies g^3 = 125 \implies g = 5$, hence the answer is C.

11. **Answer: A**

    Get the total commission by multiplying the total bouquets sold and the commission for each bouquet sold: $15 \times \$3.25 = \$48.75$, then add her monthly salary: $\$48.75 + \$100 = \$148.75$, hence the answer is A.

12. **Answer: D**

    We can assume that $x - y = 7 \implies x = 7 + y$. Substitute this expression to the second equation: $2(7 + y) + y = 8 \implies 14 + 2y + y = 8 \implies 3y = 8 - 14 \implies 3y = -6\ y = -2$. Now that we have the value of y, substitute it to $x = 7 + y \implies x = 7 + (-2) \implies x = 5$. Add the value of x and y: $5 + (-2) = 3$, hence the answer is D.

13. **Answer: B**

    Let x be the 18th score. We need to get the total scores first by multiplying the mean and the number of test scores: $83 \times 17 = 1{,}411$. Subtract 2 then from the mean: $83 - 2 = 81$. It is given that the mean (average) of a data set is found by adding all numbers in the data set and then dividing by the number of values in the set, so: $(1{,}411 + x) \div 18 = 81 \implies 1{,}411 + x = 1{,}458 \implies x = 47$, hence the answer is B.

14. **Answer: C**

    It is given that the perimeter of an isosceles triangle is $P = 2x + y$. For the first triangle: $P = 2(18) + 12 = 36 + 12 = 48$. For the second triangle: $P = 3(2) + 2 = 6 + 2 = 8$. The ratio is 48:8 or 6:1, hence the answer is C.

15. **Answer: A**

    Substitute x with 5: $k(5) = |5^4 - 5^2| = |625 - 25| = |600| = 600$, hence the answer is A.

16. Answer: **D**

It is given that a prime number is a whole number greater than 1 that cannot be exactly divided by any whole number other than itself and 1. If a number is divisible by 4, it will have a factor of 2, hence the answer is D.

17. Answer: **A**

The total bags of snack JM bought is 13. To get the percentage of the bags of Lays, $\left(\dfrac{\text{number of bags}}{\text{total number of bags}}\right) \times 100\% = \dfrac{5}{13} \times 100\% = 34.46\%$, hence the answer is A.

18. Answer: **A**

It is given that the slope-intercept form of a line is $y = mx + b$, in which b is the value of y when $x = 0$ and m is the slope. We need to get the value of b first by substituting the slope and the point: $4 = 4(4) + b \implies 4 = 16 + b \implies b = -12$. Now that we have the value of b, substitute it to the slope-intercept form $0 = 4x - 12 \implies -4x = -12 \implies x = 3$, hence the answer is A.

19. Answer: **C**

Let x be the miles, $3x$ be the miles she runs, and $5x$ be the miles she walks. $3x + 5x = 40 \implies 8x = 40 \implies x = 5$ miles. Substitute: $5x = 5(5) = 25$ miles, hence the answer is C.

20. Answer: **A**

Divide the expression: $459.84 \div 35.42 = 12.98$, hence the answer is A.

21. Answer: **A**

To evaluate, apply the PEMDAS rule. Do the parenthesis first: $24 - 6^2 \div 9 + 3 = 24 - 6^2 \div 12$. Then, the exponent: $24 - 36 \div 12$. Divide and subtract next: $24 - 3 = 21$, hence the answer is A.

22. Answer: **C**

It is given that the volume of cone is $V = \pi r^2 \dfrac{h}{3}$, in which r is the radius of the base and h is the height. To get the radius, divide the diameter by 2, so we get $r = 2$. $V = \pi 2^2 \dfrac{12}{3} = \pi(4)(4) = 16\pi$, hence the answer is C.

23. Answer: **A**

The pair factors of 429 are (1, 429), (3, 143), (11, 39), (13, 33) so its prime factors are $3 \times 11 \times 13$, hence the answer is A.

24. Answer: **C**

If a diagonal is drawn through a rectangle, it creates two right triangles. That diagonal line will be opposite to the right angle which makes it a hypotenuse. To get the hypotenuse: $c = \sqrt{a^2 + b^2} \implies c = \sqrt{9^2 + 12^2} \implies c = \sqrt{81 + 144} \implies c = \sqrt{225} \implies c = 15$, hence the answer is C.

25. **Answer: D**

    It is given that the area of a square is $A = s^2$ and the perimeter is $P = 4s$. To get the length of the side, we need to get the square root of the area: $\sqrt{289} = \sqrt{s^2} \Longrightarrow s = 17$ ft. Now that we have the side, solve for the perimeter: $P = 4(17) = 68$ ft, hence the answer is D.

26. **Answer: B**

    One way to get the greatest common factor of a given set is to list all the factors of the number.

    12 = 1, 2, 3, 4, 6, 12

    30 = 1, 2, 3, 5, 6, 10, 15, 30

    48 = 1, 2, 3, 4, 6, 8, 12, 16, 24, 48

    The greatest common factor of the three numbers is 6, hence the answer is B.

27. **Answer: A**

    One way to get least common multiple of a given set is to list the multiples of each number until at least one common multiple appears

    8 = 8, 16, 24, 32, 40

    20 = 20, 40

    The least common multiple of 8 and 20 is 40, hence the answer is A.

28. **Answer: D**

    It is given that any non-zero number raised to the power of zero is equal to one. $\dfrac{30}{15^0 - 10^0} = \dfrac{30}{1 - 1} = \dfrac{30}{0}$. It is also given that any number divided by 0 is undefined, hence the answer is D.

29. **Answer: A**

    The factors of –21 that has a sum of –4 are 3 and –7. So, $x^2 - 4x - 21 = (x + 3)(x - 7)$: $x = -3$ and $x = 7$, hence the answer is A.

30. **Answer: C**

    Combine like terms. There are two terms with x^2y: $2x^2y + x^2y$, two terms with xy^2: $-5xy^2 + (-4xy^2)$, and one term with xy: $3xy$. Simplify: $3x^2y - 9xy^2 + 3xy$, hence the answer is C.

31. **Answer: D**

    Get the extra sales from his weekly quota: total sales – weekly quota = $21,000 – $15,000 = $6,000. Multiply his commission to the extra sales: $6,000 \times \dfrac{10}{100} = 600, then add it to his weekly salary: $1,700 + $600 = $2,300, hence the answer is D.

32. Answer: **B**

   There are a total of 40 balls in the box. The probability of getting the first blue ball is $\frac{9}{40}$ and since one ball was already removed, the probability of getting the second blue ball will be $\frac{8}{39}$. Multiply: $\frac{9}{40} \cdot \frac{8}{39} = \frac{3}{65}$, hence the answer is B.

33. Answer: **B**

   There are a total of 40 balls in the box. The probability of getting a red ball is $\frac{12}{40}$ and since one ball was already removed, the probability of getting a green ball will be $\frac{10}{39}$. Multiply: $\frac{12}{40} \cdot \frac{10}{39} = \frac{4}{52}$, hence the answer is B.

34. Answer: **D**

   There are a total of 40 balls in the box. The probability of getting a yellow ball is $\frac{9}{40} = 0.225 \times 100\% = 22.5\%$, hence the answer is D.

35. Answer: **A**

   Distribute $-2x$ and we will get: $4x^2 - 14x$, hence the answer is A.

36. Answer: **B**

   Find the common factor by dividing the next two numbers: $256 \div 64 = 4$, $1{,}024 \div 256 = 4$, then multiply the common factor to the first number: $4 \times 4 = 16$, hence the answer is B.

37. Answer: **C**

   Expand: $\dfrac{\left(x^2+y^2\right)\left(x^2+y^2\right)-\left(x^2-y^2\right)\left(x^2-y^2\right)}{x^4 y^4} = \dfrac{\left(x^4+x^2y^2+x^2y^2+y^4\right)-\left(x^4-x^2y^2-x^2y^2+y^4\right)}{x^4 y^4} =$

   $\dfrac{\left(x^4+2x^2y^2+y^4\right)-\left(x^4-2x^2y^2+y^4\right)}{x^4 y^4} = \dfrac{x^4+2x^2y^2+y^4-x^4+2x^2y^2-y^4}{x^4 y^4} = \dfrac{4x^2y^2}{x^4y^4} = \dfrac{4}{x^2y^2}$, hence the answer is C.

38. Answer: **B**

   It is given that the mean (average) of a data set is found by adding all numbers in the data set and then dividing by the number of values in the set, so $\dfrac{5+4+7+6+5+2+5+4+5+9+3}{11} = \dfrac{55}{11} = 5$, hence the answer is B.

39. Answer: C

    It is given that mode is the number that occurs most often in a data set. Arrange the numbers: 2, 3, 4, 4, 5, 5, 5, 5, 6, 7, 9. Number 5 has four counts, which is the most count, hence the answer is C.

40. Answer: C

    It is given that median is the middle number in an ordered data set. Arrange the numbers: 2, 3, 4, 4, 5, 5, 5, 5, 6, 7, 9, the sixth number which is in the middle position is 5, hence the answer is C.

41. Answer: D

    Multiply: $60 \times \dfrac{175}{100} = 60 \times 1.75 = 105$, hence the answer is D.

42. Answer: B

    To get the hypotenuse: $c = \sqrt{a^2 + b^2} \implies c = \sqrt{8^2 + 6^2} \implies c = \sqrt{64 + 36} \implies c = \sqrt{100} \implies c = 10$, hence the answer is B.

43. Answer: B

    It is given that the perimeter of a pentagon is $P = 5s$. 95 cm = $5s$ s = 19 cm, hence the answer is B.

44. Answer: B

    Add the duration that Soo took to complete her homework to the time she started: 6:45 + 1:57 = 7:102 = 8:42 p.m., hence the answer is B.

45. Answer: D

    Let x be Thelma's age, $x - 5 = \dfrac{x + 8}{2} \implies 2(x - 5) = x + 8 \implies 2x - 10 = x + 8 \implies x = 18$ years old, hence the answer is D.

46. Answer: A

    When multiplying two expressions with the same base, we apply the rule, $a^x \cdot a^y = a^{x+y}$, in which "a" is the common base and "x" and "y" are the exponents. $b^{4+3+2} = b^9$, hence the answer is A.

47. Answer: A

    Multiply: $\dfrac{1}{10} \times \dfrac{3}{5} \times \dfrac{5}{2} = \dfrac{15}{100} = \dfrac{3}{20}$, hence the answer is A.

For the ISEE, the most commonly referenced score is the stanine score. Check out the four steps to calculating stanine scores.

Step 1: The Raw Score

The first step in scoring is calculating a raw score. This is quite simple.

Students receive one point for each correct answer and no points for incorrect answers or unanswered questions.

Tip: Because there is no score penalty for incorrect answers or unanswered questions, be sure to answer every single question! Answering all of the questions can only increase your chances of a higher score.

Step 2: The Scaled Score

Once a raw score has been calculated for each section, it is converted into a scaled score.

This conversion adjusts for the variation in difficulty between different tests. Thus, a lower raw score on a harder test could give you the same scaled score as a higher raw score on an easier test. This process is called equating.

The scaled score for each section ranges from 760 to 940.

Step 3: The Percentile Score

Next, the percentile score for each section is calculated.

Percentiles compare a student's scaled score to all other same-grade students from the past three years. This is important to understand because the ISEE is taken by students in a range of grades. The Upper Level ISEE, for instance, is taken by students applying to grades 9–12; however, the percentile score is based only on the performance of other students applying to the same grade. Thus, a student applying to 9th grade will not be compared to a student applying to 12th grade.

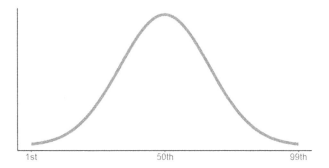

1st   50th   99th

Here's an example to help understand percentile scores: scoring in the 40th percentile indicates that a student scored the same or higher than 40% of students in the same grade but lower than 59% of students.

Step 4: The Stanine Score

Finally, the percentile is converted into a stanine score.

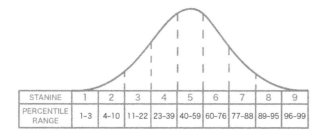

STANINE	1	2	3	4	5	6	7	8	9
PERCENTILE RANGE	1-3	4-10	11-22	23-39	40-59	60-76	77-88	89-95	96-99

Notice that the percentile ranges for the middle stanines of 4–6 are far larger than the ranges for the extreme stanines of 1, 2, 8, or 9. This means that most students taking the ISEE achieve scores in the middle ranges. Only the top 4% of all test takers receive a stanine of 9 on any given section, while 20% of students receive a stanine of 5.

So, what is a good ISEE score?

Stanine scores (which range from 1 to 9) are the most important and are the scores schools pay the most attention to. But what is a good score on the ISEE? A score of 5 or higher will be enough to put students in the running for most schools, although some elite private schools want applicants to have ISEE test results of 7 or higher.

Here's a sample ISEE Report

Individual Student Report

Candidate for Grade	**8**
ID Number	
Gender	**Male**
Date of Birth	**4/8/2004**
Phone Number	
Test Level/Form	**Middle/0916**
Date of Testing	**11/30/2016**
Tracking Number	**201612010592103**

The Test Profile below shows your total scores for each test. Refer to the enclosed brochure called *Understanding the Individual Student Report* to help you interpret the *Test Profile* and *Analysis*. Percentile Ranks and Stanines are derived from norms for applicants to independent schools.

TEST PROFILE

Section	Scaled Score (760 – 940)	Percentile Rank (1 – 99)	Stanine (1 – 9)	Stanine Analysis 1 2 3 4 5 6 7 8 9
Verbal Reasoning	895	90	8	V
Reading Comprehension	890	76	6	R
Quantitative Reasoning	894	81	7	Q
Mathematics Achievement	883	61	6	M

LEGEND: V = Verbal Reasoning R = Reading Comprehension Q = Quantitative Reasoning M = Mathematics Achievement

ANALYSIS

Section & Subsection	# of Questions	# Correct	Results for each Question
Verbal Reasoning			
Synonyms	18	15	++++++++- ++++- ++.- +
Single Word Response	17	16	+++++++++++- +++++
Quantitative Reasoning			
Word Problems	18	11	+++- - - +++- +++++- - -
Quantitative Comparisons	14	14	++++++++++++++
Reading Comprehension			
Main Idea	4	4	++++
Supporting Ideas	6	5	- +++++
Inference	6	5	+- ++++
Vocabulary	7	5	+++- +- +
Organization/Logic	4	4	++++
Tone/Style/Figurative Language	3	3	+++
Mathematics Achievement			
Whole Numbers	7	4	+- +++- -
Decimals, Percents, Fractions	9	5	++- - ++- - +
Algebraic Concepts	11	7	+++++- ++- - -
Geometry	4	2	+- +-
Measurement	5	4	++++-
Data Analysis and Probability	6	4	+++- +-

LEGEND: + = Correct - = Incorrect S = Skipped N = Not Reached

The test was administered in the order reported in the analysis section; Verbal Reasoning, Quantitative Reasoning, Reading Comprehension, and Mathematics Achievement. Each section was divided into subsections, grouping similar types of questions. The Reading Comprehension subsection grouping does not represent the actual order of the test questions.

The above is a preliminary ISEE report. ERB reserves the right to amend this report before it is finalized. The report will be final no later than 20 business days. The final report will automatically be generated electronically.

ISEE—Upper Level Exam-2

Verbal Reasoning

You have 20 minutes to answer the 40 questions in the Verbal Reasoning Section.

This section is divided into two parts that contain two different types of questions. As soon as you have completed Part I, answer the questions in Part II. You may write in your test booklet. For each answer you select, fill in the corresponding circle on your answer document.

Part I—Synonyms

Each question in Part I consists of a word in capital letters followed by four answer choices. Select the one word that is most nearly the same in meaning as the word in capital letters.

SAMPLE QUESTION: <u>Sample Answer</u>

CHARGE: A   B   ●   D

(A) release
(B) belittle
(C) accuse
(D) conspire

Part II—Sentence Completion

Each question in Part II is made up of a sentence with one blank. Each blank indicates that a word or phrase is missing. The sentence is followed by four answer choices. Select the word or phrase that will best complete the meaning of the sentence as a whole.

SAMPLE QUESTIONS: <u>Sample Answer</u>

It rained so much that the streets were _____.   ●   B   C   D

(A) flooded
(B) arid
(C) paved
(D) crowded

The house was so dirty that it took _____.   A   B   C   ●

(A) less than 10 min to wash it
(B) four months to demolish it
(C) over a week to walk across it
(D) two days to clean it

Part I—Synonyms

Directions:

Select the word that is most nearly the same in meaning as the word in capital letters.

1. CHAGRIN:

   (A) delight   (B) amusement   (C) surprise   (D) vexation

2. PARSIMONIOUS:

   (A) generous   (B) extravagant   (C) stingy   (D) wasteful

3. ABRIDGE:

   (A) expand   (B) abbreviate   (C) extend   (D) elongate

4. ABSTRUSE:

   (A) obscure   (B) clear   (C) simple   (D) straightforward

5. BURGEON:

   (A) flourish   (B) slow   (C) dwindle   (D) deplete

6. DEPRECATE:

   (A) approve   (B) criticize   (C) admire   (D) agree

7. FLORID:

   (A) plain   (B) simple   (C) elaborate   (D) humble

8. ILLUMINE:

   (A) delude   (B) darken   (C) secret   (D) enlighten

9. OBVIATE:

   (A) slide   (B) let   (C) allow   (D) avert

10. SECEDE:

(A) join (B) split (C) affiliate (D) register

11. COLLOQUIAL:

(A) formal (B) informal (C) business (D) foreign

12. GUMPTION:

(A) stupidity (B) ignorance (C) ingenuity (D) folly

13. ODIOUS:

(A) delightful (B) impressive (C) loathsome (D) handsome

14. RETICENT:

(A) discreet (B) aggressive (C) fighter (D) talkative

15. TEMERITY:

(A) audacity (B) silence (C) humility (D) shame

16. ACCOLADE:

(A) tribute (B) punishment (C) criticism (D) hate

17. BEDLAM:

(A) peace (B) chaos (C) serenity (D) harmony

18. ECLECTIC:

(A) singular (B) diverse (C) union (D) unique

19. ONEROUS:

(A) simple (B) easy (C) light (D) tedious

20. RECTITUDE:

(A) immorality (B) scandalous (C) integrity (D) dishonest

Part II—Sentence Completion

Directions:

Select the word that best completes the sentence.

21. In this age where the world is at _____, world peace, as an answer to pageant questions, is not meaningless anymore.

    (A) order   (B) turmoil   (C) stability   (D) harmony

22. If you keep up this _____ abysmal performance, the university will be forced to kick you out of the scholarship so find a way.

    (A) abysmal   (B) superb(C) exceptional   (D) top

23. The _____ businessman hides in his mansion after many disappointed customers came to get their money back for receiving counterfeit items.

    (A) confident   (B) craven   (C) proud   (D) honest

24. Christy's parents could not believe that they were invited to the principal's office for her bad attendance and for _____ the school rules.

    (A) adhering   (B) obeying   (C) flouting   (D) advocating

25. No matter how many times John's parents lecture him, he never seems to _____ their teachings and proceeds to make mischief.

    (A) deflect   (B) reject   (C) oppose   (D) imbibe

26. The class enjoyed the _____ of performing without proper practice until they saw how well done others' performance were.

    (A) wisdom   (B) prudence   (C) discretion   (D) folly

27. I cannot forget the _____ remarks he told me before. So, I will not let him inside my circle now.

    (A) delightful   (B) alluring   (C) odious   (D) pleasant

28. In addition to leather being _____ which makes it easy to work with, it also lasts a lifetime because of its durability.

    (A) huge   (B) pliable   (C) critical   (D) negligible

29. There are several _____ wars all over the word that are not known to many. It is sad to think that there are cries that nobody hears about.

(A) virulent (B) benevolent (C) genial (D) cordial

30. Do not believe in everything you see online. Most of them are _____.

(A) canards (B) truth (C) facts (D) proven

31. Someone's most _____ memory is _____ his happiest or saddest.

(A) memorable ... both (B) forgettable ... either (C) indelible ... either

(D) unremarkable ... neither

32. _____ on your studies instead on _____ basketball teens who have yet to prove anything.

(A) sleep ... stout (B) ignore ... handsome (C) focus ... lanky (D) slack ... smart

33. Mother always throws _____ questions at the dinner table. They are most often about school so do not _____ to lie.

(A) intelligent ... fret (B) rhetorical ... dare (C) silly ... restrain (D) funny ... curb

34. Daphne was told to keep her _____ behavior to herself and avoid any form of _____ while the relatives are in town.

(A) dignified ... recognition (B) uncouth ... embarrassment (C) decent ... collision

(D) elegant ... argument

35. Joseph left the board of his own _____ to _____ his writing and moved to the countryside.

(A) duty ... escape (B) pressure ... avoid (C) duress ... stop (D) volition ... pursue

36. After a few months, you'll _____ and learn the _____ of the locals.

(A) doubt ... tongue (B) defend ... order (C) repulse ... rules (D) acclimate ... ways

37. He spoke a few _____ words then _____ into doing his work so he can leave early for the weekend.

(A) flattering ... cajoled (B) disgusting ... harassed (C) nasty ... pestered (D) lewd ... compelled

38. She was always considered _____ of the boys because of her _____ behavior.

(A) none ... manly (B) out ... gentle (C) one ... brusque (D) among ... girly

39. We always wondered how she knew about _____ matters and could understand _____ languages.

(A) arcane ... ancient (B) trivial ... modern (C) simple ... alien (D) easy ... local

40. It is _____ knowledge that the Sun is the _____ of the Solar System.

(A) universal ... edge (B) ecumenical ... center (C) local ... center (D) limited ... bottom

End of section.

If you have any time left, go over the questions in this section only.

Do not start the next section.

Quantitative Reasoning

You have 35 minutes to answer the 37 questions in the Quantitative Reasoning Section.

Each question is followed by four suggested answers. Read each question and then decide which one of the four suggested answers is best.

Find the row of spaces on your document that has the same number as the question. In this row, mark the space having the same letter as the answer you have chosen. You may write in your test booklet.

EXAMPLE 1:   Sample Answer

What is the value of the expression (4 + 6) ÷ 2?   A   B   ●   D

(A) 2
(B) 4
(C) 5
(D) 7

The correct answer is 5, so circle C is darkened.

EXAMPLE 2:

A square has an area of 25 cm². What is the length of one of its   A   ●   C   D
side?

(A) 1 cm
(B) 5 cm
(C) 10 cm
(D) 25 cm

The correct answer is 5 cm, so circle B is darkened.

Part I—Word Problems (20 QS)

Each question in Part I is consisting of a word problem followed by four answer choices. Look at the four answer choices given and select the best answer.

1. Mica is an uprising actress. She has increased her Twitter following of 1,200 by 35%. How many followers does she now have?

   (A) 1,620   (B) 1,600   (C) 1,610   (D) 1,590

2. Dara, Cheol, and Marlo were tasked to buy for an event. Cheol has bought three times as many flowers as Marlo and Dara has bought 20 more flowers than Cheol. They bought a total of 55 flowers. How many flowers did Dara bought?

   (A) 30   (B) 45   (C) 40   (D) 35

3. One businessman earns $19,750 per year. Another businessman earns $1,720 per month. How much more does the second businessman make in a year than the first businessman?

   (A) $850   (B) $890   (C) $900   (D) $875

4. Two numbers add to 2,400. One number is seven times the size of the other. What are the two numbers?

   (A) 300 and 2,100   (B) 400 and 2,000   (C) 200 and 2,200   (D) 500 and 1,900

5. A box of laundry soap contains 300 oz. If the cost for 5 oz is 8 cents, how much does the box of soap cost?

   (A) $4.00   (B) $4.50   (C) $4.80   (D) $4.20

6. The number of fourth-grade students in the Hill School is 8 more than $\frac{1}{6}$ of the whole student body. If there are 144 students in the school, how many are in fourth grade?

   (A) 25   (B) 3   (C) 32   (D) 35

7. A clock is showing 9:00. What is the measure of the angle formed by the hour and minute hands?

   (A) 95°   (B) 180°   (C) 120°   (D) 90°

8. A rectangular play area measures 28 yards by 17 yards. What would be the perimeter?

   (A) 84 yards   (B) 90 yards   (C) 87 yards   (D) 92 yards

9. Harry is four times as old as his brother James at present. After 10 years he will be twice the age of his brother. Find Harry's current age.

   (A) 5 years old   (B) 10 years old   (C) 15 years old   (D) 20 years old

10. If the sum of two consecutive numbers is equal to 97, what are the numbers?

(A) 48 and 49   (B) 47 and 48   (C) 46 and 47   (D) 49 and 50

11. An oil container contains $7\frac{1}{2}$ liters of oil which are poured into $2\frac{1}{2}$ liters bottles. How many bottles are needed to fill $7\frac{1}{2}$ liters of oil?

(A) 2 bottles   (B) 3 bottles   (C) 4 bottles   (D) 5 bottles

12. In a right triangle, the legs are 6 ft long and 8 ft long. How long is the hypotenuse?

(A) 7 ft   (B) 9 ft   (C) 10 ft   (D) 12 ft

13. If a heptagon has a perimeter of 119 in, assuming that the sides are equal, how long is each side?

(A) 17 in   (B) 15 in   (C) 20 in   (D) 18 in

14. A baker sells chocolate packets that contain 15 chocolates and biscuit packet that has 9 biscuits. What is the least number of chocolates and biscuits Zoe should buy so that there will be one biscuit for every chocolate?

(A) 40   (B) 38   (C) 50   (D) 45

15. Layla brought a box that contains green and purple balls in the ratio of 3:5 green to purple, how many purple balls are there if 90 green balls are in the box?

(A) 150   (B) 140   (C) 130   (D) 120

16. At an annual rate of $0.50 per $100, what is the annual fire insurance premium for a house that is insured for $75,000?

(A) $350.00   (B) $325.00   (C) $375.00   (D) $340.00

17. What is the value of a positive number if the square of that number minus the number is equal to 72?

(A) –9   (B) 9   (C) –8   (D) 8

18. Kellie finished $\frac{2}{3}$ of a book. She still needs to read 90 more pages. How long is her book?

(A) 240 pages long   (B) 250 pages long   (C) 260 pages long   (D) 270 pages long

19. In a group of 120 people, 90 have an age of more 30 years, and the others have an age of less than 20 years. If a person is selected at random from this group, what is the probability the person's age is less than 20?

(A) 25%   (B) 20%   (C) 27%   (D) 22%

20. Which digit is in the tenths place in the number 615.97?

(A) 6   (B) 1   (C) 9   (D) 7

Part II—Quantitative Comparison (17 QS)

All questions in Part II are quantitative comparisons between the quantities shown in Column A and Column B. Using the information given in each question, compare the quantity in Column A to the quantity in Column B, and choose one of these four answer choices:

(A) the quantity in Column A is greater

(B) the quantity in Column B is greater

(C) the two quantities are equal

(D) the relationship cannot be determined from the information given

1. $11 \times 6(7 + x) = 1$

Column A	Column B
The value of x	The value of y

2.

Column A	Column B
$\dfrac{3}{5}$ of 100	$\dfrac{1}{2}$ of 120

For questions 3 and 4, please refer to the figure below:

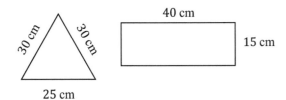

3.

Column A	Column B
Perimeter of the triangle	Perimeter of the rectangle

4.

Column A	Column B
Longest side of rectangle	Longest side of the rectangle

5. Let $x = 12$, $y = 7$, $z = 9$

Column A	Column B
$x + yz$	$3x(16y - 2z)$

6. Let $3 > b > -5$

Column A	Column B
$\dfrac{2}{b}$	$\dfrac{b}{2}$

For questions 7 and 8, please refer to the rectangle MATR below:

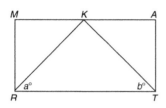

7. Assuming that $a < b$

Column A	Column B
Line KR	Line KT

8.

Column A	Column B
Line RT	Line MA

9. Let p be an integer

Column A	Column B
p^4	p^5

10.

Column A	Column B
$(3 \times 2) + 29 - 11$	$2^2 + (12 \div 3) - 1$

11.

Column A	Column B
60% of 160	45% of 280

12.

Column A	Column B
$\sqrt[3]{729}$	$\sqrt[4]{625}$

13.

Column A	Column B
$\dfrac{2}{3} + \dfrac{2}{3} + \dfrac{2}{3}$	$\dfrac{9}{2}$

14.

Column A	Column B
The side of a square if the perimeter is 16	5

15. Let $g = 1$

Column A	Column B
$g^5 + g^2 - g - 1$	$g^8 - g^4 + g^2 - 1$

16.

Column A	Column B
Perimeter of a square if each side is 25 ft	Perimeter of a pentagon if each side is 20 ft

17.

Column A	Column B
Area of a circle if the radius is m^3	Area of a circle if the radius is $3m$

End of section.

If you have any time left, go over the questions in this section only.

Do not start the next section.

You have 35 minutes to answer the 36 questions in the Reading Comprehension and Vocabulary section.

Directions:

This section contains six short reading passages. Each passage is followed by six questions based on its content. Answer the questions following each passage on the basis of what is stated or implied in that passage. You may write in your test booklet.

Questions 1–6

In recent months, many public universities have restricted access to TikTok on school computers, mobile phones and Wi-Fi, in accordance with executive orders in those states banning the app on government-owned devices and networks.

Governors have cited cybersecurity issues and fears over Chinese spying as reasons for the bans. States like Maryland prohibited the app and other Chinese and Russian products on Dec. 6, after an investigation by NBC News revealed that a state-sponsored hacking group stole millions in unemployment money from the U.S.

A few days later, on Dec. 13, lawmakers in the U.S. House and Senate proposed a bipartisan bill to ban TikTok federally. Bills to block the app on state devices in California, Massachusetts, New York, and Vermont have also been proposed. As states continue to restrict TikTok, some public universities have barred access to the platform on campus in order to cooperate with the law, leaving students frustrated.

A TikTok spokesperson previously told NBC News the company is "disappointed that so many states are jumping on the political <u>bandwagon</u>."

"We're especially sorry to see the unintended consequences of these rushed policies beginning to impact universities' ability to share campus-wide information, recruit students, and build communities around athletic teams, student groups, campus publications, and more," TikTok spokesperson Brooke Oberwetter said in an e-mail statement in December.

1. What is the main topic of the passage?

   (A) promoting the ban of TikTok

   (B) information regarding universities banning TikTok to cooperate with the law

   (C) disapproval on banning of TikTok

   (D) proving that TikTok does not impose security threat

2. According to the passage, what caused the TikTok ban?

   (A) students earning more money thus leaving universities   (B) students failing their grades

   (C) bullying   (D) cybersecurity issues and fears over Chinese spying

3. True or false. The passage states that TikTok will be banned on all devices and networks across the U.S.

   (A) true   (B) false   (C) maybe   (D) not known

4. How did the students react when public universities barred access to TikTok on campus?

   (A) not affected   (B) delighted   (C) focused more on studies   (D) frustrated

5. What does the underlined word in line 5 mean?

   (A) prohibit   (B) permit   (C) allow   (D) approve

6. What does the underlined word in line 27 mean?

   (A) vehicle   (B) cart   (C) trend   (D) prohibition

Questions 7–12

Exercise enhances your body, mind, and mood.

Maybe you exercise to tone your thighs, build your biceps, or flatten your belly. Or maybe you work out to ward off the health conditions, like heart disease, diabetes, and cancer.

There are many benefits to exercise, but how about sweating to improve your mind?

"Exercise is the single best thing you can do for your brain in terms of mood, memory and learning," says Dr. John Ratey, author of the book, "Spark: The Revolutionary New Science of Exercise and the Brain," and an associate clinical professor of psychiatry at Harvard Medical School. "Even 10 minutes of activity changes your brain."

If you need a little extra <u>incentive</u> to lace up those sneakers and get moving, here are a few <u>mind-blowing</u> benefits and ways exercise can boost your brainpower and overall health:

Staves off the aging process
Helps lift depression and anxiety
Recharges your spirit
Improves learning
Raises functional ability
Promotes fun and enjoyment
Leaves you feeling euphoric
Fosters confidence
Clears your head space
Keeps the brain fit
May keep dementia at bay
Helps you process emotions

7. What is the main topic of the passage?

(A) encourage readers to sign up for a gym membership

(B) discourages readers to exercise as it does not significantly help your health

(C) share benefits of exercise to your brainpower and overall health

(D) information that exercise only impacts your physical health

8. What does it mean to feel euphoric?

(A) feel physically exhausted   (B) improved mood and feel positive   (C) feel sleepy   (D) feel depressed

9. What does the underlined word in line 4 mean?

(A) embrace   (B) welcome   (C) attracts   (D) fight

10. What does the underlined word in line 16 mean?

(A) motivation   (B) deterrent   (C) cash   (D) curb

11. What does the underlined word in line 18 mean?

(A) dull   (B) tedious   (C) thrilling   (D) humdrum

12. How many minutes does someone need to get benefits from exercise?

(A) not stated in the passage   (B) 1 hr   (C) 1 min   (D) 10 min

Questions 13–18

It's completely normal for everyone to get an upset stomach from time to time, and there are various reasons behind it.

"It could be a meal that didn't agree with you for whatever reason," says Keri Gans, a registered dietitian based in New York City. "It could be stress, nerves or it could just be a 24-hour bug."

Studies have shown a connection between the brain and the gut that links mood and anxiety to digestion, but stomach troubles can also be caused by parasites, food allergies and sensitivities.

For generations, many pediatricians and parents have recommended the BRAT diet—which stands for bananas, rice, applesauce, and toast —to remedy upset stomachs. However, the American Academy of Pediatrics changed its recommendation in the late 1990s after understanding that the BRAT diet lacked key nutrients—such as fiber, calcium, protein, fat, and vitamin B12—to help children recover. This dispelled the popular myth that people experiencing vomiting, nausea and diarrhea should restrict their eating.

Instead, experts say a healthy, well-balanced diet is better for recovery than the highly restrictive BRAT diet. This generally applies to adults, as well.

Fortunately, there are certain foods you can eat when you have an upset stomach that should help you feel better.

Here are 13 foods that are good to eat for an upset stomach:

Apple cider vinegar
Broth-based soups
Crackers (plain)
Dry white toast
Ginger
Other herbs and spices such as chamomile, licorice, spearmint, and mint
White rice
Unseasoned, skinless chicken, turkey, or fish
Oatmeal
Sugarless gum
Unsweetened applesauce
Yogurt

13. What is the main topic of the passage?

(A) medical advice that people with upset stomach must restrict their eating

(B) information on what food can help an upset stomach

(C) promote BRAT diet for upset stomach

(D) promote sales of bananas in the supermarket

14. What is the BRAT diet?

(A) bananas, rice, applesauce, and toast   (B) diet for spoiled kids

(C) effective way to lose weight   (D) a form of fasting

15. What caused the pediatricians to change their recommendations for upset stomach instead of BRAT?

(A) it made children's stomach more upset   (B) it made people fat

(C) they found out that the diet lacked key nutrients to help children recover

(D) it caused a higher demand on bananas, rice, applesauce, and toast

16. True or false. Someone with upset stomach must restrict their eating to avoid upsetting the stomach even more.

(A) maybe   (B) true   (C) false   (D) not known

17. What is the meaning of the underlined word in line 7?

(A) insect   (B) a fly   (C) program error   (D) virus

18. What is the meaning of the underlined word in line 22?

(A) engender   (B) banish   (C) promote   (D) flourish

Questions 19–24

The updated COVID-19 booster shot that targets two omicron subvariants as well as the original coronavirus strain has been available to most Americans for over four months, but the Centers for Disease Control and Prevention says just 18% of adults have gotten it.

So why have so few people rolled up their sleeves?

Despite COVID-19 deaths in the U.S. once again being on the rise, the months-long booster campaign appears to have an education problem, according to a report published Thursday by the CDC.

The most common reason given for not getting the updated COVID-19 booster shot was a lack of knowledge about eligibility for it, according to researchers.

The survey, which was conducted in early November, asked 1,200 vaccinated Americans their reasons for receiving or not receiving an updated booster shot. Of the 714 Americans who had not yet gotten the updated shot, more than 23%—or close to 1 in 4—reported that they did not know they were eligible for it.

The second most common reason was a lack of knowledge about vaccine availability, while the third most commonly reported reason was a perceived <u>belief</u> that they were already protected against infection.

Most participants who were unaware they were eligible for the shot planned to get the booster after reviewing information about vaccination guidelines, the survey found. But a month later, only 29% of the participants who planned to receive the shot had done so, with recontacted participants reporting they were too busy, forgot or worried about the side effects.

Lack of knowledge about the updated booster shot is not a new trend. A survey published in September found that half of the U.S. had heard little or nothing about the new shots—an issue the researchers behind Thursday's report also address.

"Increasing awareness is a crucial first step toward increasing coverage; promotion of tools that provide vaccination guidance by public health authorities and trusted messengers might help encourage persons who are unsure about bivalent booster dose recommendations to receive the booster dose," they said.

19. What is the main topic of the passage?

(A) information on why many Americans have not availed the booster shot

(B) data on how many COVID-19 variants are in circulation

(C) information when and where to get booster shots

(D) requirements on how to avail booster shot

20. What were the reasons for the low penetration rate of booster shot on Americans?

(A) they did not know they were eligible for it   (B) lack of knowledge about vaccine availability

(C) perceived belief that they were already protected against infection   (D) all of the above

21. How many participated in the survey on their reasons for receiving or not receiving an updated booster shot conducted in early November?

(A) 1,200 vaccinated Americans   (B) 714   (C) 23%   (D) 18%

22. What were the reasons why only 29% of the participants got their booster shot?

(A) too busy   (B) forgot   (C) worried about the side effects   (D) all of the above

23. What can be done to improve the penetration rate of the booster shot on Americans?

(A) make it federally required for all   (B) incentivize the booster shot with cash

(C) increase awareness, promote tools on vaccination guidelines, and messengers to help encourage people

(D) none of the above

24. What does the underlined word in line 28 mean?

(A) doubt   (B) opinion   (C) fact   (D) truth

Questions 25–30

Across the country, patients who had certain procedures, such as joint replacement and cancer surgery, were disproportionately white. These procedures are usually elective, meaning they are scheduled in advance. Only 29% of hospitals in the analysis treated a proportion of Black patients that was comparable to or higher than the proportion of Black residents in the community. And only 18% and 5% of hospitals met that bar for Hispanic and Asian/Pacific Islander patients, respectively.

These are among the findings of an initiative by U.S. News, publisher of the Best Hospitals rankings, to measure health equity across U.S. hospitals and the communities they serve. Results have been published on hospital profiles at usnews.com/best-hospitals. Because of data limitations, relatively few hospitals could be evaluated for equitable access for Native Americans. In addition, the term Hispanic is used in this article because the administrative claims data in the analysis categorize Medicare beneficiaries' ethnicity as Hispanic or other.

Multiple causes may account for the racial and ethnic differences the data reveal, and intentional discrimination isn't necessarily involved. Researchers have proposed that decreased access to health care, patient-doctor communication barriers, lack of trust and other factors may contribute to communities of color receiving less of certain types of elective care.

The analysis also found:

In many communities, Medicare-insured residents who are Black, compared to similarly insured residents of other races, have experienced more hospitalizations that might have been avoidable if they'd had access to better preventive health care. These potentially preventable hospitalizations reflect missed opportunities to improve the health of thousands, if not millions, of American residents. Preventable hospitalizations also impose a high financial cost on U.S. taxpayers, whose dollars support Medicare. Conditions leading to the hospitalizations include uncontrolled diabetes, congestive heart failure and chronic obstructive pulmonary disease.

While some communities made progress over time toward closing the racial gap in potentially preventable hospitalizations, that gap remained stubbornly persistent in many parts of the country—and it grew worse since 2011 in nearly a third of U.S. communities, despite incentives for hospitals in the 2010 Affordable Care Act to invest in improving the health of local populations.

25. What is the main topic of the passage?

(A) information on why racial gaps exist in hospital care

(B) proof that racial discrimination exists even in hospital care

(C) convince readers to get medical care from hospitals and clinics run by the same race

(D) data that whites get hospitalized more compared to other races

26. True or false. Intentional racial discrimination is the top reason for the racial gaps in hospital care according to the study.

(A) not stated   (B) true   (C) false   (D) maybe

27. What are the factors that contribute to racial gap according to the study?

(A) decreased access to health care   (B) patient–doctor communication barriers

(C) lack of trust   (D) all of the above

28. What were the leading conditions that caused hospitalizations which could have prevented if they'd had access to better preventive care?

(A) uncontrolled diabetes   (B) congestive heart failure   (C) chronic obstructive pulmonary disease

(D) all of the above

29. What does the underlined word in line 11 mean?

(A) altogether   (B) for each person or thing   (C) collectively

(D) with everyone or everything taken into account at the same time

30. What does the underlined word in line 19 mean?

(A) fair   (B) biased   (C) partial   (D) prejudiced

Questions 31–36

College students may be classified as "nontraditional" because of their age or employment status, or because they have one or more dependents, are independent for financial aid, are enrolled part time or don't have a traditional high school diploma, among other reasons, according to the National Center for Education Statistics.

Before choosing a college, nontraditional students should make an "honest assessment of what they are looking for from an educational experience and what they can fit in their current lives," Kaleba says.

Experts advise nontraditional students to ask questions throughout the application process, including whether they would qualify for priority registration or what kind of support services are available on campus. Most colleges have a library, career services and a financial aid office, but not all schools provide resources to help with childcare, transportation, or basic needs insecurities.

Additionally, nontraditional students should remember that a bachelor's degree at a four-year institution is not the only option. Depending on their career goals, students can seek out an associate degree or shorter-term, industry-recognized credentials and certificates.

Once enrolled, don't be afraid to ask for help both inside and outside the classroom.

Make sure that faculty and administrators are aware of the challenges you're facing, such as needing childcare support, transportation, food or housing assistance, or test-taking accommodations, Kaleba says.

31. What is the main topic of passage?

(A) advise for nontraditional college students on how they can effectively go thru college with the assistance that may be available for them

(B) discourage nontraditional students to go back to school

(C) convince readers that a college degree is not a sure ticket to success

(D) promote which schools' nontraditional student may go

32. Which among the choices below are considered nontraditional college students?

(A) older than the average college student   (B) with dependents   (C) working   (D) all of the above

33. What could be the possible reasons why a nontraditional college student may need test-taking accommodations based on its definition?

(A) they may be lazy because of old age

(B) they may need help in their busy schedule due to work or childcare

(C) they may often get sick

(D) because they may need extra help to understand lectures

34. True or false. Not all schools provide resources to help with childcare, transportation, or basic needs insecurities which is why it's important that nontraditional students assess their needs before choosing a university.

(A) true   (B) false   (C) maybe, there is no telling for sure   (D) not stated in the passage

35. Which among the words below is a synonym of the underlined word in line 16?

(A) not considered   (B) late   (C) urgency   (D) back burner

36. What does the underlined word in line 26 mean?

(A) ignore   (B) veer   (C) discriminate   (D) attain

End of section.

If you have any time left, go over the questions in this section only.

Do not start the next section.

You have 40 minutes to answer the 47 questions in the Mathematics Achievement Section.

Each question is followed by four suggested answers. Read each question and then decide which one of the four suggested answers is best.

Find the row of spaces on your document that has the same number as the question. In this row, mark the space having the same letter as the answer you have chosen. You may write in your test booklet.

SAMPLE QUESTION: Sample Answer

Which of the numbers below is not factor of 364?   A ● C D

(A) 13
(B) 20
(C) 26
(D) 91

The correct answer is 20, so circle B is darkened.

---

1. The measures of the angles of a nine-sided polygon, or nonagon, form an arithmetic sequence. The least of the nine-degree measures is 127°. What is the greatest of the nine-degree measures?

    (A) 153°   (B) 160°   (C) 162°   (D) 155.5°

2. What is the value of 19.25 – 3.47?

    (A) 15.87   (B) 15.78   (C) 14.92   (D) 14.29

3. The legs of a right triangle are equal to 7 and 10. What is the length of the hypotenuse?

    (A) $\sqrt{159}$ (B) $\sqrt{169}$ (C) $\sqrt{139}$ (D) $\sqrt{149}$

4. If $a - b = 8$, then which expression is equal to b?

(A) $-a - 8$ (B) $a - 8$ (C) $a + 8$ (D) $-a + 8$

For questions 5–7, please refer to the chart below:

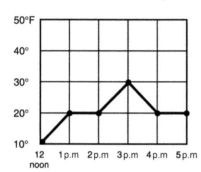

Temperature data last Monday

5. At what time is the recorded highest temperature?

(A) 4:00 p.m. (B) 3:00 a.m. (C) 3:00 p.m. (D) 3:30 p.m.

6. What was the recorded temperature at 1:30 p.m.?

(A) 20°C (B) 30°C (C) 15°F (D) 20°F

7. What was the recorded temperature at 5:00 a.m.?

(A) 20°F (B) 10°F (C) 30°F (D) no available data

8. The circumference of a circle is 12.56 in. Find the area of the circle. Let $\pi = 3.14$.

(A) 11 in² (B) 11.56 in² (C) 12.56 in² (D) 12 in²

9. Solve for the value of h: $5h - 12 = 33$.

(A) 9 (B) 8 (C) 7 (D) 6

10. The manager at Jessica's Furniture Store is trying to figure out how much to charge for a couch that just arrived. The couch was bought at a wholesale price of $152.00 and Jessica's Furniture Store marks up all furniture by 35%.

(A) $202.50 (B) $202.70 (C) $205.20 (D) $205.50

11. Zyra travels at the rate of 60 mph and covers 300 miles in 5 hr. If she reduces her speed by 10 mph, how long will she take to cover the same distance?

(A) 6 hr (B) 5 hr (C) 7 hr (D) 4 hr

12. What is the sum of all the factors of 40?

(A) 89   (B) 90   (C) 85   (D) 93

13. Simplify: $2a^3 - 3a^2 + 7a^2 - 10a^3$

(A) $-4a^2(-2a + 1)$ (B) $4a^2(2a - 1)$ (C) $-4a^2(2a - 1)$ (D) $-4a^2(2a^2 - 1)$

For questions 14–16. Please refer to the given data.

- The median of 15 consecutive integers in a set of data is 67.

14. What is the smallest integer in the set of data?

(A) 58   (B) 59   (C) 60   (D) 61

15. What is the highest integer in the set of data?

(A) 73   (B) 74   (C) 72   (D) 71

16. What is the mean in the set of data?

(A) 65   (B) 68   (C) 72   (D) 67

17. Which of the following can be the next number after 37 in the sequence below?
{1, 2, 5, 10, 17, 26, 37, ...}

(A) 45   (B) 50   (C) 40   (D) 55

18. Give the x-intercept of the line of the equation $7x + 3y = 210$.

(A) (0, 30)   (B) (0, 70)   (C) (70, 0)   (D) (30, 0)

19. The College of Engineering has 800 students. If 75% of them are boys, how many girls are there?

(A) 200   (B) 210   (C) 190   (D) 195

20. Solve for x in this equation:

$$\frac{5-2}{\sqrt{x}} = \frac{3}{4}$$

(A) 10   (B) 15   (C) 12   (D) 16

21. Miranda is Chloe's mother. Miranda is 42 years old. Seven years ago, Miranda was seven times as old as her daughter was then. How old is Chloe now?

(A) 11 years old   (B) 10 years old   (C) 12 years old   (D) 9 years old

22. When four times a number is increased by 16, the result is 256. Find the number.

(A) 55   (B) 60   (C) 65   (D) 70

23. A small square is located inside a bigger square. The length of one side of the small square is 5 in and the length of one side of the big square is 9 in. What is the area of the region located outside the small square, but inside the big square?

A) 56 in²   B) 52 in²   C) 58 in²   D) 53 in²

24. Find the perimeter of a heptagon with a side having a length of 12 cm.

(A) 80 cm   (B) 84 cm   (C) 70 cm   (D) 72 cm

25. Last year, Ling earned $200 a month at her part-time job as a barista. This year, her earnings have increased to $280 per month. What is the percent increase in her monthly earnings?

(A) 30%   (B) 35%   (C) 40%   (D) 45%

26. Evaluate the expression: 15,975.358 − 21,275.67 + 385.79 + 42.452

(A) 4,872.07   (B) 4,827.70   (C) −4,872.07   (D) −4,827.04

27. Solve the expression: $\dfrac{9a^{10}b^7c^3}{3a^8b^5c^2}$

(A) $\dfrac{3a^2b^2c}{a^2b}$ (B) $3a^2b^2c$ (C) $\dfrac{a^2b^2c}{3}$ (D) $3abc$

For questions 28–31, please refer to the graph below:

Kris works in a multimedia company and her monthly salary is $700. To avoid overspending on the things she doesn't need, she makes sure to follow her monthly budget.

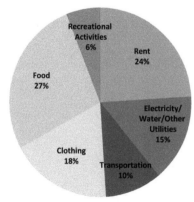

Kris's Monthly Budget

28. What percentage of Kris's salary does she spend on housing costs?

(A) 23%   (B) 12%   (C) 66%   (D) 39%

29. How much does she spend on her hobbies and entertainment?

(A) $42   (B) $34   (C) $49   (D) $30

30. How much does she spend on food and clothing?

(A) $303   (B) $315   (C) $289   (D) $385

31. How much did she allocate for transportation?

(A) $85   (B) $75   (C) $80   (D) $70

32. The sum of two numbers is 23. The difference of the same two numbers is 5. What are the two numbers?

(A) 14 and 9   (B) 14 and 7   (C) 13 and 10   (D) 13 and 8

33. What is 140% of 90?

(A) 126   (B) 148   (C) 114   (D) 135

34. Janell wants to replace the glass in her rectangular mirror. She can buy glass for $0.75 per square inch. How much would she pay if the mirror has a dimension of 36 in by 17 in?

(A) $439.50   (B) $449.00   (C) $459.00   (D) $475.50

35. One number exceeds another number by 18. If the sum of the two numbers is 82, find the smaller number.

(A) 30   (B) 29   (C) 37   (D) 32

36. The sum of three consecutive integers is 438. What is the largest integer?

(A) 145   (B) 147   (C) 146   (D) 148

37. How much simple interest will an account earn in three years if $230 is invested at 8% interest per year?

(A) $50.20   (B) $53.50   (C) $52.55   (D) $55.20

38. Evaluate: $3^3 + (15 + 3) - (2 \times 7) + 19$

(A) 48   (B) 49   (C) 50   (D) 51

39. If a box contains purple and yellow balls in the ratio of 3:4 purple to yellow, how many purple balls are there if 80 yellow balls are in the box?

(A) 50 (B) 65 (C) 55 (D) 60

40. Simplify the expression: $5x^2y^3 + 10x^3y^5 - (3x^2y^3 - x^3y^5)$

(A) $3x^2y^3 + 11x^3y^5$ (B) $2x^2y^3 + 11x^3y^5$ (C) $3x^2y^3 - 11x^3y^5$ (D) $2x^2y^3 - 11x^3y^5$

41. What is 95% of 4,620?

(A) 4,398 (B) 4,893 (C) 4,389 (D) 4,983

For questions 42–43, please refer to the figure below:

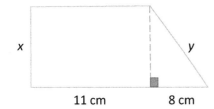

42. If the area of the trapezoid above is 90 cm², what is the value of x?

(A) 6 cm (B) 7 cm (C) 8 cm (D) 9 cm

43. Using the same area in question 42, how long is y?

(A) 8.49 cm (B) 8 cm (C) 9.48 cm (D) 10 cm

44. If $\dfrac{7}{a} = \dfrac{b}{8}$, the

(A) $ab = 56$ (B) $\dfrac{b}{a} = \dfrac{7}{8}$ (C) $\dfrac{a}{b} = \dfrac{8}{7}$ (D) $ab = 65$

45. Simplify: $g^{14} \div g^{10}$

(A) g^{24} (B) g^{14} (C) g^4 (D) g^{10}

46. Find the sum of the inferior angles of a regular nonagon.

(A) 1620° (B) 1260° (C) 1026° (D) 1602°

47. In a decagon, each of the 10 sides is equal to one another. If the perimeter is 243 ft, what is the length of one of the sides?

(A) 23.4 ft (B) 24.2 ft (C) 23.2 ft (D) 24.3 ft

End of section.

If you have any time left, go over the questions in this section only.

Do not start the next section.

ANSWER KEY

Verbal Reasoning

1.	D	7.	C	13.	C	19.	D	25.	D	31.	C	37.	B
2.	C	8.	D	14.	A	20.	C	26.	D	32.	C	38.	C
3.	B	9.	D	15.	A	21.	B	27.	C	33.	B	39.	A
4.	A	10.	B	16.	A	22.	A	28.	B	34.	B	40.	B
5.	A	11.	B	17.	B	23.	B	29.	A	35.	D		
6.	B	12.	C	18.	C	24.	C	30.	A	36.	D		

ISEE UL Verbal 1

1. The correct answer is (D). Chagrin means strong feelings of embarrassment. Synonyms are humiliation, vexation, and mortification.

2. The correct answer is (C). When someone is parsimonious, he is excessively unwilling to spend. Synonyms are stingy, frugal, and thrifty.

3. The correct answer is (B). To abridge means to shorten something. Synonyms are to condense, abbreviate, and reduce.

4. The correct answer is (A). Abstruse means difficult to understand. Synonyms are obscure, puzzling, and complex.

5. The correct answer is (A). To burgeon means to grow rapidly. Synonyms are to multiply, flourish, and prosper.

6. The correct answer is (B). To deprecate means to express disapproval of something. Synonyms are to criticize, condemn, and belittle.

7. The correct answer is (C). Florid means excessively intricate or complicated. Synonyms are ornate, elaborate, and fancy.

8. The correct answer is (D). To illumine is to enlighten someone. Synonyms are light up and brighten.

9.   The correct answer is (D). To obviate means to remove a need or a difficulty. Synonyms are to avoid, prevent, and avert.

10. The correct answer is (B). To secede means to formally withdraw from a membership. Synonyms are to separate, split, and break away.

11. The correct answer is (B). Colloquial means used in everyday conversation. Synonyms are informal, conversational, and slang.

12. The correct answer is (C). Gumption means spirited initiative and resourcefulness. Synonyms are imagination, ingenuity, and wit.

13. The correct answer is (C). Odious means arousing or deserving hatred. Synonyms are horrible, abhorrent, and loathsome.

14. The correct answer is (A). Reticent means not expressive or feeling or thought. Synonyms are cagy, discreet, and restrained.

15. The correct answer is (A). Temerity means excessive boldness or confidence. Synonyms are audacity, nerve, and impudence.

16. The correct answer is (A). An accolade is an award or a praise. Synonyms are tribute, honor, and compliment.

17. The correct answer is (B). Bedlam is a scene of uproar and confusion. Synonyms are mayhem, chaos, and disorder.

18. The correct answer is (C). Eclectic means deriving from a wide variety of sources. Synonyms are varied, extensive, and diverse.

19. The correct answer is (D). Onerous means oppressively burdensome. Synonyms are arduous, tiring, and tedious.

20. The correct answer is (C). Rectitude means morally correct behavior or thinking. Synonyms are righteousness, integrity, and decency.

21. The correct answer is (B). Turmoil means chaos. The speaker is saying that world peace is not a meaningless answer to pageant questions anymore because of the chaos all over the world.

22. The correct answer is (A). Abysmal means terrible. The speaker is saying that if the person keeps up his terrible performance, he'll lose his scholarship.

23. The correct answer is (B). Craven means cowardly. In this sentence, the cowardly businessman went into hiding and did not face his disappointed customers.

24. The correct answer is (C). To flout means to defy. In this sentence, Christy's parents were invited to the principal's office for her bad attendance and for defying the school rules.

25. The correct answer is (D). To imbibe means to take in or up or drink. In this sentence, John never takes in his parents' lectures and continues to make trouble.

26. The correct answer is (D). Folly refers to a foolish action, practice, idea, etc., absurdity. In this sentence, they enjoyed fooling around and did not practice until they saw that other's performance were well done.

27. The correct answer is (C). Odious means highly offensive; repugnant; disgusting. In this sentence, the speaker cannot forget his offensive remarks which is why she will not be friends with him.

28. The correct answer is (B). Pliable means supple enough to bend freely or repeatedly without breaking. In this sentence, because leather is pliable, it is easy to work with. In addition, leather is durable.

29. The correct answer is (A). Virulent means intensely bitter, spiteful, or malicious. In this sentence, there are several spiteful wars happening around the world that a lot of people do not know about.

30. The correct answer is (A). Canard means a false or baseless, usually derogatory story, report, or rumor. In this sentence, the speaker is warning someone to not believe everything they see online as most of them are false.

31. The correct answer is (C). Indelible means not easily forgotten; memorable. In this sentence, someone's most memorable memory is either his happiest one or saddest.

32. The correct answer is (C). Lanky means ungracefully thin and rawboned; bony; gaunt. In this sentence, the speaker is telling someone to focus on her studies instead on tall thin basketball teens.

33. The correct answer is (B). Rhetorical means asked merely for effect with no answer expected. In this sentence, mother is known to ask rhetorical questions about school at the dinner table, so you are warned to not lie. Most probably, mother already knows the answer.

34. The correct answer is (B). Uncouth means awkward and uncultivated in appearance, manner, or behavior: rude. In this sentence, Daphne was reprimanded to behave while the relatives are in town.

35. The correct answer is (D). Volition means the power of choosing or determining: will. In this sentence, Joseph left at his own will and moved to the countryside to pursue his writing.

36. The correct answer is (D). To acclimate means to accustom or become accustomed to a new climate or environment: adapt. In this sentence, the speaker tells us that after a few months, you'll adapt and learn the ways of the locals.

37. The correct answer is (B). To cajole means to get (someone) to do something by gentle urging, special attention, or flattery.

38. The correct answer is (C). Brusque means abrupt in manner; blunt; rough.

39. The correct answer is (A). Arcane means known or understood by very few; mysterious; secret; obscure; esoteric.

40. The correct answer is (B). Ecumenical means worldwide or general in extent, influence, or application.

Quantitative Reasoning

WORD PROBLEMS		QUANTITATIVE COMPARISONS	
1. A	11. B	1. D	11. B
2. D	12. C	2. C	12. A
3. B	13. A	3. B	13. B
4. A	14. D	4. A	14. B
5. C	15. A	5. B	15. C
6. C	16. C	6. D	16. C
7. D	17. B	7. A	17. D
8. B	18. D	8. C	
9. D	19. A	9. D	
10. A	20. C	10. A	

Part I—Word Problems (20 QS)

1. Answer: **A**

   Multiply her previous follower count with the increase in percentage: $1,200 \times \dfrac{35}{100} = 420$. Then add it to the previous following: $1,200 + 420 = 1,620$. Hence, the answer is A.

2. Answer: **D**

    Let x be the number of flowers bought by Marlo. Let $3x$ be the number of flowers bought by Cheol since she bought three times more than Marlo and $3x + 20$ for Dara. Add then the number of flowers: $x + 3x + 3x + 20 = 55 \implies 7x = 35 \implies x = 5$. Substitute: $3(5) + 20 = 35$. Hence, the answer is D.

3. Answer: **B**

    It is given that there are 12 months in a year. Multiply the second businessman's monthly income by 12 months to get his annual income. $\$1,720 \times 12 = \$20,640$. Subtract it then to with the first businessman's annual income: $\$20,640 - \$19,750 = \$890$, hence the answer is B.

4. Answer: **A**

    Let x be the first number. Add the two numbers: $x + 7x = 2,400 \implies 8x = 2,400 \implies x = 300$. We have now the value of the first number. Then multiply the first number with seven to get the second one: $7(300) = 2,100$, hence, the answer is A.

5. Answer: **C**

    Divide 300 by 5: $300 \div 5 = 60 \times 0.08$ cents $= \$4.80$, hence, the answer is C.

6. Answer: **C**

    Get $\dfrac{1}{6}$ of the total student body: $144 \times \dfrac{1}{6} = 24 + 8 = 32$, hence the answer is C.

7. Answer: **D**

    At 9:00 the hour and minute hands on a clock form a right angle, which measures 90°, hence the answer is D.

8. Answer: **B**

    It is given the perimeter of rectangle is $P = 2l + 2w$. $P = 2(28) + 2(17) = 56 + 34 = 90$ yards, hence the answer is B.

9. Answer: **D**

	Current Age	Age after 10 Years
Harry	$4x$	$4x + 10$
James	x	$x + 10$

    It is given that in 10 years, Harry will be twice as old as James: $4x + 10 = 2(x + 10) \implies 4x + 10 = 2x + 20$

    $\implies 2x = 10 \implies x = 5$. We now have the value of x which is James' current age. To get Harry's current age, multiply 4 to James' current age: $4(5) = 20$ years old. Hence the answer is D.

10. **Answer: A**

    Let x be the first number and $x + 1$ for the second number. Write the equation: $x + x + 1 = 97 \implies$

    $2x = 96 \implies x = 48$. The first number is 48, since the numbers are consecutive, just add 1 for the second number: $48 + 1 = 49$, hence the answer is A.

11. **Answer: B**

    Let x be the number of bottles. $2\frac{1}{2}x = 7\frac{1}{2} \implies 2.5x = 7.5 \implies x = 3$ bottles, hence the answer is B. $\implies$

12. **Answer: C**

    It is given that hypotenuse $(c) = \sqrt{a^2 + b^2} \implies c = \sqrt{6^2 + 8^2} = \sqrt{36 + 64} = \sqrt{100} = 10$, hence the answer is C.

13. **Answer: A**

    Heptagon is a polygon that has seven sides. To get the length of side, divide the perimeter with 7: $119 \div 7 = 17$ in, hence the answer is A.

14. **Answer: D**

    We need to find the LCM to know how many chocolates and biscuits Zoe needs to buy. One way to get the LCM is through listing.

    $15 = 15, 30, 45$

    $9 = 9, 18, 27, 36, 45$

    The LCM is 45, hence the answer is D.

15. **Answer: A**

    Let x be the number of purple balls. We can write a proportion to solve: $\frac{3}{5} = \frac{90}{x}$, then cross multiply: $3x = 450 \implies x = 150$, hence the answer is A.

16. **Answer: C**

    Let's first determine how many \$100 there are in \$75,000: $\frac{75,000}{100} = 750$, then multiply it with the annual rate: $750 \times \$0.50 = \$375.00$. The annual insurance premium is \$375.00 hence the answer is C.

17. **Answer: B**

    Let x be the number. Write the equation: $x^2 - x = 72$. Subtract 72 on both sides: $x^2 - x - 72 = 0$. Factor the left-hand side: $(x + 8)(x - 9) = 0$. Thus, $x = 9$ or -8. As the question indicated that x is a positive number, $x = 9$, hence the answer is B.

18. Answer: **D**

    Let x be the total number of pages. She read $\frac{2}{3}$ of the book: $x - \frac{2}{3}x = \frac{1}{3}x$ pages left to read. $\frac{1}{3}x = 90 \implies$ $x = 270$ pages long, hence the answer is D.

19. Answer: **A**

    We need first to get the number of people whose age is less than 20: 120 – 90 = 30.

    Probability that a person selected at random from the group is less than 20 is given by 30 ÷ 120 = 0.25 × 100% = 25, hence the answer is A.

20. Answer: **C**

    It is given that the first digit after decimal represents the tenths place, hence the answer is C.

Part II—Quantitative Comparison (17 QS)

1. Answer: **D**

   There's not enough data to get the value of y. We can only solve the value of x, hence the answer is D.

2. Answer: **C**

   The word "of" after a fraction indicates multiplication. In column A: $\frac{3}{5} \times 100 = 60$, In column B: $\frac{1}{2} \times 120 = 60$. Both columns have the same value, hence the answer is C.

3. Answer: **B**

   It is given that the perimeter of triangle is $P = a + b + c$ for non-equilateral triangle.

   $P = 30 + 30 + 25 \implies P = 85$ cm. To find the perimeter of rectangle, it is given, $P = 2l + 2w$.

   $P = 2(40) + 2(15) \implies P = 110$ cm. The perimeter of the rectangle is greater than that of the triangle, hence the answer is B.

4. Answer: **A**

   The longest side of the rectangle is 40 cm while the longest side of the triangle is 30 cm. Forty centimeters is greater than 30 cm, hence the answer is A.

5. Answer: **B**

   Substitute with the given value. $x + yz = 12 + (7 \times 9)$. Apply the PEMDAS rule. There's no exponent, so solve the equation on the parenthesis first, then add: 12 + 63 = 75. Do the same for Column B: (3 × 12) [(16 × 7) – (2 × 9)] = (36) (112 – 18) = (36) (94) = 3,384, hence the answer is B.

6. Answer: **D**

Since *b* could be any nonzero value between 3 and –5, the values of the fractions will vary. There's not enough data to determine which column is greater, hence the answer is D.

7. Answer: **A**

There's a given that b° is greater than a°. The opposite of the greater angle is the longer line, hence the answer A.

8. Answer: **C**

It is given the opposite sides of a rectangle are equal and parallel. In the figure, rectangle MATR, line RT, and line MA are opposite, thus they are equal. The answer is C.

9. Answer: **D**

There's not enough data to determine which column is greater. *P* can be any integer. If we substitute 1 to the value of *p*, both columns will have the same value. If we substitute any positive integer (aside from 1) to the value of *p*, Column B will be greater but if we substitute any negative integer, column A will be greater, hence the answer is D.

10. Answer: **A**

To evaluate the expressions, apply the PEMDAS rule. Solve first the parenthesis: (3 × 2) + 29 – 11 = 6 + 29 – 11. There's no exponent, multiplication, and division, so add and subtract from left to right: 6 + 29 – 11 = 24. Do the same with column B. Solve first for the parenthesis and exponent: 2^2 + (12 ÷ 3) – 1 = 4 + 4 – 1, then add and subtract from left to right: 4 + 4 – 1 = 7. Twenty-four is greater than 7, hence the answer is A.

11. Answer: **B**

The word "of" after a percent sign indicates multiplication. In column A: $\frac{60}{100}$ × 160 = 96. In column B: $\frac{45}{100}$ × 280 = 126. One hundred and twenty-six is greater than 96, hence the answer is B.

12. Answer: **A**

Evaluate the expressions. The cube root of 729 is 9, while the fourth root of 625 is 5. Nine is greater than 5, hence the answer is A.

13. Answer: **B**

Evaluate the expression on Column A: $\frac{2}{3} + \frac{2}{3} + \frac{2}{3} = \frac{6}{3} = 2$. The decimal value of $\frac{9}{2}$ is 4.5 which is greater than 2, hence the answer is B.

14. Answer: **B**

It is given that the perimeter of a square is $P = 4s \implies 16 = 4s \implies s = 4$. Five is greater than 4, hence the answer is B.

15. Answer: C

It is given that $g = 1$, Substitute it on the expressions. In Column A: $g^5 + g^2 - g - 1 = 1^5 + 1^2 - 1 - 1 = 1 + 1 - 1 - 1 = 0$. In Column B, $g^8 - g^4 + g^2 - 1 = 1^8 - 1^4 + 1^2 - 1 = 1 - 1 + 1 - 1 = 0$, both columns have the same value, hence the answer is C.

16. Answer: C

It is given that the perimeter of a square is $P = 4s \implies P = 4(25) = 100$ ft. For the perimeter of a pentagon, it is given $P = 5s \implies P = 5(20) = 100$ ft. Both columns have the same value, hence the answer is C.

17. Answer: D

There's not enough data to determine the area of each column. There's no value given for m, hence the answer is D.

Reading Comprehension and Vocabulary

1.	B	7.	C	13.	B	19.	A	25.	A	31.	A
2.	D	8.	B	14.	A	20.	D	26.	C	32.	D
3.	A	9.	D	15.	C	21.	A	27.	D	33.	B
4.	D	10.	A	16.	C	22.	D	28.	D	34.	A
5.	A	11.	C	17.	D	23.	C	29.	B	35.	C
6.	C	12.	D	18.	B	24.	B	30.	A	36.	D

ISEE UL Reading 3

1. The correct answer is (B). See lines 1–6, 20–25.

2. The correct answer is (D). See lines 7–9.

3. The correct answer is (A). See lines 5–6, 22–24. The passage states that TikTok will be banned on government-owned devices and networks. Some public universities have barred access to the platform on campus to cooperate with the law.

4. The correct answer is (D). See lines 24–25.

5. The correct answer is (A). To ban means officially or legally prohibit.

6. The correct answer is (C). Bandwagon refers to a popular party, faction, or a cause that attracts growing support. It can be a current or fashionable trend.

7. The correct answer is (C).

8. The correct answer is (B). Euphoric means experiencing or marked by overwhelming usually pleasurable emotion. Passage states that one of the benefits of exercise is improving your mood.

9. The correct answer is (D). To ward (off) means to guard, protect.

10. The correct answer is (A). Incentive is a thing that motivates or encourages one to do something.

11. The correct answer is (C). Mind-blowing means overwhelmingly impressive.

12. The correct answer is (D). See lines 14–15.

13. The correct answer is (B). See lines 31–33.

14. The correct answer is (A). See lines 15–16.

15. The correct answer is (C). See lines 17–21.

16. The correct answer is (C). See lines 22–27. The passage states that the statement is a myth.

17. The correct answer is (D). Bug in this sentence means a harmful microorganism, as a bacterium or virus.

18. The correct answer is (B). To dispel means to make (a doubt, feeling, or belief) disappear.

19. The correct answer is (A). See lines 5–6, 9–13.

20. The correct answer is (D). See lines 25–33.

21. The correct answer is (A). See line 19.

22. The correct answer is (D). See lines 36–41.

23. The correct answer is (C). See lines 47–54.

24. The correct answer is (B). Belief means something one accepts as true or real; a firmly held opinion or conviction.

25. The correct answer is (A). See lines 27–38.

26. The correct answer is (C). According to the analysis, multiple causes may account for the racial gap and intentional discrimination isn't necessarily involved. See lines 29–31.

27. The correct answer is (D). See lines 27–37.

28. The correct answer is (D). See lines 44–52.

29. The correct answer is (B). Respectively means separately or individually and in the order already mentioned (used when enumerating two or more items or facts that refer to a previous statement).

30. The correct answer is (A). Equitable means marked by justice, honesty, and freedom from bias.

31. The correct answer is (A). The passage talks about what noncollege students must consider and do so they can make most out of being back in college and where to get help for possible challenges they may face such as childcare support, transportation, test-taking accommodations.

32. The correct answer is (D). See lines 2–7.

33. The correct answer is (B). As outlined by the National Center for Education Statistics, college students may be classified as nontraditional because employment status, or because they have one or more dependents. This makes choice B a reasonable answer.

34. The correct answer is (A). See lines 9–13, 20–22.

35. The correct answer is (C). Priority means the right to one's attention before other things considered less important.

36. The correct answer is (D). To seek (out) means to attempt or desire to obtain or achieve (something).

Mathematics Achievement

1. A	11. A	21. C	31. D	41. C
2. B	12. B	22. B	32. A	42. A
3. D	13. C	23. A	33. A	43. D
4. B	14. C	24. B	34. C	44. A
5. C	15. B	25. C	35. D	45. C
6. D	16. D	26. C	36. B	46. B
7. D	17. B	27. B	37. D	47. D
8. C	18. D	28. D	38. C	
9. A	19. A	29. A	39. D	
10. C	20. D	30. B	40. B	

1. Answer: **A**

    We need first to get the total degree of the nonagon. The total degree of a polygon is measured through the formula $180° (n - 2)$, where n is the number of sides of the polygon. Nonagon has nine sides, so substitute n with 9: $180° (9 - 2) = 180° (7) = 1260°$.

    Next, in an arithmetic sequence, the terms are separated by a common difference, which we will call d. Since the least of the degree measures is 127°, the measures of the angles are 127°, 127° + d, 127° + $2d$, ..., 127° + $8d$. Solve for their sum: 127°, 127° + d, 127° + $2d$, ..., 127° + $8d$ = 1260° 1143° + $36d$ = 1260° $\implies$ $36d = 117°$ $\implies$ d = 3.25. Now that we have the value of d, substitute it to the 127° + $8d$ = 127° + 8(3.25) = 127° + 26 = 153°, hence the answer is A.

2. Answer: **B**

    Subtract: 19.25 – 3.47 = 15.78, the answer is B.

3. Answer: **D**

    To get the hypotenuse, we use $c = \sqrt{a^2 + b^2}$. Substitute the values of a and b with the given dimensions: $c = \sqrt{7^2 + 10^2}$ $\implies$ $c = \sqrt{49 + 100}$ $\implies$ $c = \sqrt{149}$, hence the answer is D.

4. Answer: **B**

    We first need to subtract a from both sides: $-b = 8 - a$. Next, divide both sides by –1: $b = -8 + a$ (or $a - 8$), hence the answer is B.

5. **Answer: C**

The recorded highest temperature last Monday was 30°F which was recorded at 3:00 p.m., hence the answer is C.

6. **Answer: D**

1:30 p.m. is between 1:00 p.m. and 2:00 p.m. The recorded temperature 1:00 p.m.–2:00 p.m. is 20°F, hence the answer is D.

7. **Answer: D**

There's no data provided for the temperature last Monday morning. The given data is only for 12:00 noon–5:00 p.m., hence the answer is D.

8. **Answer: C**

We need first to find the radius of the circle. The circumference of a circle is $c = 2\pi r$, where r is the radius of the circle. It is given that $\pi = 3.14$: $12.56 = 2 \times 3.14 \times r \Longrightarrow 6.28r = 12.56 \Longrightarrow r = 2$ in. Next, get the area by using the formula: $A = \pi r^2 = 3.14 \times 2^2 = 3.14 \times 4 = 12.56$ in^2, hence the answer is C.

9. **Answer: A**

Evaluate the given expression: $5h - 12 = 33 \Longrightarrow 5h = 33 + 12 \Longrightarrow 5h = 45 \Longrightarrow h = 9$, hence the answer is A.

10. **Answer: C**

The keyword "marks up" indicates that the manager will be adding 35% to the wholesale price. We need to get the amount of the price increase, first. Multiply the percent to the wholesale price: 35% or $\frac{35}{100} \times \$152.00 = \$53.20$, then add this amount to the original price: $\$152.00 + \$53.20 = \$205.20$, hence the answer is C.

11. **Answer: A**

The original speed is 60 mph. If the speed is reduced by 10 mph, then the new speed will be 50 mph. It was given that the distance is 300 miles. To get the new time to cover this distance, we will use the formula: $\text{time} = \dfrac{\text{distance}}{\text{speed}} = \dfrac{300\,\text{miles}}{50\,\text{mph}} = 6$ hr, hence the answer is A.

12. **Answer: B**

List all the factors of 40: 1, 2, 4, 5, 8, 10, 20, 40, then add: $1 + 2 + 4 + 5 + 8 + 10 + 20 + 40 = 90$, hence the answer is B.

13. Answer: C

Rearrange the expression with like terms: $2a^3 - 10a^3 - 3a^2 + 7a^2$. Combine like terms: $-8a^3 + 4a^2$. Find the common factor: $-4a^2(2a - 1)$, hence the answer is C.

14. Answer: C

We know that the numbers should be arranged in ascending order to find the median. When the number of the given data is odd, the median is the single middle value. In this question we have 15 consecutive integers with the median of 67. So, the median is the eighth number in the rearranged data set. Since the 15 integers are consecutive, then the smallest integer is seven less than the median: $67 - 7 = 60$, hence the answer is C.

15. Answer: B

Getting the highest integer is similar on how we got the smallest integer but instead of subtracting seven from the median, we will be adding seven: $67 + 7 = 74$, hence the answer is B.

16. Answer: D

Mean is the average of the set of values. To get the mean, we need to add all numbers in the data set and then divide it by the number of values in the set:

$$\frac{60 + 61 + 62 + 63 + 64 + 65 + 66 + 67 + 68 + 69 + 70 + 71 + 72 + 73 + 74}{15} = \frac{1,005}{15} = 67,$$ hence the answer is D.

17. Answer: B

The succeeding numbers in the sequence are the result of adding consecutive odd numbers on the preceding number: $1 + 1 = 2$, $2 + 3 = 5$, $5 + 5 = 10$, $10 + 7 = 17$, $17 + 9 = 26$, $26 + 11 = 37$, $37 + 13 = 50$, hence the answer is B.

18. Answer: D

Let $y = 0$: $7x + 3(0) = 210 \implies 7x = 210 \implies x = 30$, the x-intercept is $(30, 0)$, hence the answer is D.

19. Answer: A

Let x be the number of girls. Since 75% of the students are boys, the remaining 25% will be girls. We can set up the following proportion: $\frac{25}{100} = \frac{x}{800}$, then cross multiply: $100x = 20,000 \implies x = 200$, hence the answer is A.

20. Answer: D

To solve the expression, apply cross multiplication: $\frac{5-2}{\sqrt{x}} = \frac{3}{4} \implies 3\sqrt{x} = 4(5 - 2) \implies 3\sqrt{x} = 4(3) \implies$ $3\sqrt{x} = 12 \implies \sqrt{x} = 4 \implies x = 16$, hence the answer is D.

21. Answer: **C**

Let x be Chloe's age.

	Current Age	Age Seven Years Ago
Miranda	42	42 – 7
Chloe	x	x – 7

It was given that seven years ago, Miranda was seven times older than Chloe, and we can express that with $42 - 7 = 7(x - 7) \implies 35 = 7x - 49 \implies -7x = -84 \implies x = 12$, Chloe is 12 years old, hence the answer is C.

22. Answer: **B**

Let x be the number. The keyword "times" indicates multiplication and "increase" denotes addition. Write the algebraic expression of the given problem and solve: $4x + 16 = 256 \implies 4x = 240 \implies x = 60$, hence the answer is B.

23. Answer: **A**

Get the area of the squares first. To get the area of a square, we need to use the formula: $A = s^2$. For the big square: $A = 9^2 = 81$ in². For the small square: $A = 5^2 = 25$ in². We need to get the area of the shaded region, and to get that, we need to subtract the area of the bigger square to the area of the small one: 81 in² – 25 in² = 56 in². The area of the shaded region is 56 in², hence the answer is A.

24. Answer: **B**

The perimeter of heptagon is $P = 7a$, where a is the length of one side. $P = 7(12 \text{ cm}) = 84$ cm, hence the answer is B.

25. Answer: **C**

To get the percent increase, we need to use the formula: $\text{percent change} = \dfrac{\text{change}}{\text{starting point}}$.

$\text{percent change} = \dfrac{\text{change}}{\text{starting point}} = \dfrac{\$280 - \$200}{\$280} = \dfrac{\$80}{\$280} = 0.40 \text{ or } 40\%$, hence the answer is C.

26. Answer: **C**

Evaluate the given operation: $15,975.358 - 21,275.67 + 385.79 + 42.452 = -4,872.07$. The answer is C.

27. Answer: **B**

To divide variables with exponents, apply the rule $x^a \div x^b = x^{a-b}$, where x is the variable and a and b are exponents. $\dfrac{9a^{10}b^7c^3}{3a^8b^5c^2} = \dfrac{9a^{10-8}b^{7-5}c^{3-2}}{3} = 3a^2b^2c$, hence the answer is B.

28. Answer: **D**

The housing costs comprise rent which is 24% and utilities expenses (electricity, water, other utilities) which is 15%. Combine these two: 24% + 15% = 39%, hence the answer is D.

29. Answer: **A**

Hobbies and entertainment are under the Recreational Activities budget with 6% allotment. Since Kris's monthly salary is $700, we need to get 6% of $700 to know how much she spends on recreational activities: $700 \times \dfrac{6}{100} = \$42$, hence the answer is A.

30. Answer: **B**

Food and clothing allotted budget are 27% and 18%, respectively. We need to get how much she spends on these from her monthly salary. $\$700 \times \dfrac{27}{100} = \$189$, $\$700 \times \dfrac{18}{100} = \$126$. Add these two: $189 + $126 = $315. She spends $315 on food and clothes, hence the answer is B.

31. Answer: **D**

Transportation has a 10% budget. We need to get 10% from $700, which is her monthly salary: $\$700 \times \dfrac{10}{100} = \$70$. She spends $70 on her transportation, hence the answer is D.

32. Answer: **A**

Let x be the first number and y be the second number. Write the algebraic expressions on the given problem. If we add the two numbers, we get: $x + y = 23$, if we subtract the two numbers, we get: $x - y = 5$. Combine the two expressions:

$$
\begin{aligned}
x + y &= 23 \\
+\ x + y &=\ \ 5 \\
\hline
2x &= 28 \\
x &= 14
\end{aligned}
$$

Now that we got the value of x which is the first number, substitute the value to any of the expressions: $x + y = 23 \implies 14 + y = 23 \implies y = 9$. The two numbers are 14 and 9, hence the answer is A.

33. Answer: **A**

The word "of" after a percent sign indicates multiplication. $\dfrac{140}{100} \times 90 = 126$, hence the answer is A.

34. Answer: **C**

We need to get first the area of the mirror. To get the area of rectangle, use the formula: $A = lw$ $A = 36 \times 17 = 612$ in². Next, multiply the area to the cost per square inch: $612 \times 0.75 = \$459$, hence the answer is C.

35. Answer: **D**

Let x be the smaller number, $x + 18$ be the second number. If we add the two numbers, we get 82: $x + x + 18 = 82 \implies 2x + 18 = 82 \implies 2x = 64 \implies x = 32$, hence the answer is D.

36. Answer: **B**

Let x be the first number, $x + 1$ the second number, and $x + 2$ the third and largest number. If we add these three numbers, we get 438: $x + x + 1 + x + 2 = 438 \implies 3x + 3 = 438 \implies 3x = 435 \implies x = 145$. We have now the value of x which is the first number. Substitute this to $x + 2$ to get the largest number: $145 + 2 = 147$, hence the answer is B.

37. Answer: **D**

To get the interest (I), we need to use this formula: interest = principal (p) × rate × time. $I = prt \implies I = 230 \times 0.08 \times 3 = 55.2$. The interest is \$55.20, hence the answer is D.

38. Answer: **C**

Apply the PEMDAS rule: Evaluate first the parentheses and exponents: $3^3 + (15 + 3) - (2 \times 7) + 19 = 27 + 18 - 14 + 19$. Since there's no multiplication and division after solving the parentheses and exponents, proceed with addition and subtraction from left to right: $27 + 18 - 14 + 19 = 50$, hence the answer is C.

39. Answer: **D**

Let x be the number of purple balls. We need to write a proportion with the given values first: $\dfrac{3}{4} = \dfrac{x}{80}$.
Next, apply cross multiplication: $4x = 240 \implies x = 60$. There are 60 purple balls, hence the answer is D.

40. Answer: **B**

Distribute first -1 to the expression inside the parenthesis: $5x^2y^3 + 10x^3y^5 - 3x^2y^3 + x^3y^5$. Rearrange the expressions with like terms: $5x^2y^3 - 3x^2y^3 + 10x^3y^5 + x^3y^5$. Combine the like terms: $2x^2y^3 + 11x^3y^5$, hence the answer is B.

41. Answer: **C**

The word "of" after a percent sign indicates multiplication. $\dfrac{95}{100} \times 4{,}620 = 4{,}389$, hence the answer is C.

42. Answer: **A**

The area of trapezoid can be solved by the using the formula: $A = \left(\dfrac{1}{2}h\right) \times (b_1 + b_2)$. The measure of the first base (b_1) is 11 cm and the second base (b_2) is 19 cm. The value of x is the height (h). We have the area of 90 cm². Substitute the values to get x: $90 = \left(\dfrac{1}{2}x\right) \times (11 + 19) \implies 90 = \left(\dfrac{1}{2}x\right) \times (11 + 19) \implies 90 = 15x \implies x = 6$, hence the answer is A.

43. Answer: **D**

    The angle opposite of line y is a right angle, so y is a hypotenuse. To solve for the hypotenuse, use the formula: $c = \sqrt{a^2 + b^2} \implies c = \sqrt{8^2 + 6^2} = \sqrt{64 + 36} = \sqrt{100} = 10$. y is 10 cm, hence the answer is D.

44. Answer: **A**

    To simplify the expression, apply cross multiplication. After we cross multiply, we will get $ab = 56$, hence the answer is A.

45. Answer: **C**

    To divide variables with exponents, apply the rule $x^a \div x^b = x^{a-b}$, where x is the variable and a and b are exponents. $g^{14} \div g^{10} = g^{14-10} = g^4$, hence the answer is C.

46. Answer: **B**

    The sum of the interior angles of a regular polygon can be solved using the equation: 180°$(n - 2)$ where n is the number of sides in the polygon. A nonagon has nine sides. 180°(9–2) = 180°(7) = 1260°. The sum of the interior angles of a nonagon is 1260°, hence the answer is B.

47. Answer: **D**

    A decagon is a 10-sided polygon. To get the perimeter, we use the formula: $P = 10s$. Substitute the value of perimeter (P) to solve for the side: 243 = 10$s \implies s = 24.3$. Each side measures 24.3 ft, hence the answer is D.

For the ISEE, the most commonly referenced score is the stanine score. Check out the four steps to calculating stanine scores.

Step 1: The Raw Score

The first step in scoring is calculating a raw score. This is quite simple.

Students receive one point for each correct answer and no points for incorrect answers or unanswered questions.

Tip: Because there is no score penalty for incorrect answers or unanswered questions, be sure to answer every single question! Answering all of the questions can only increase your chances of a higher score.

Step 2: The Scaled Score

Once a raw score has been calculated for each section, it is converted into a scaled score.

This conversion adjusts for the variation in difficulty between different tests. Thus, a lower raw score on a harder test could give you the same scaled score as a higher raw score on an easier test. This process is called equating.

The scaled score for each section ranges from 760 to 940.

Step 3: The Percentile Score

Next, the percentile score for each section is calculated.

Percentiles compare a student's scaled score to all other same-grade students from the past three years. This is important to understand because the ISEE is taken by students in a range of grades. The Upper Level ISEE, for instance, is taken by students applying to grades 9–12; however, the percentile score is based only on the performance of other students applying to the same grade. Thus, a student applying to 9th grade will not be compared to a student applying to 12th grade.

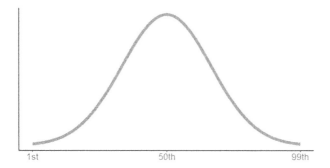

Here's an example to help understand percentile scores: scoring in the 40th percentile indicates that a student scored the same or higher than 40% of students in the same grade but lower than 59% of students.

Step 4: The Stanine Score

Finally, the percentile is converted into a stanine score.

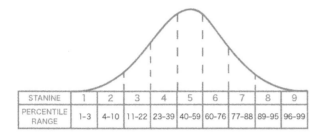

STANINE	1	2	3	4	5	6	7	8	9
PERCENTILE RANGE	1–3	4–10	11–22	23–39	40–59	60–76	77–88	89–95	96–99

Notice that the percentile ranges for the middle stanines of 4–6 are far larger than the ranges for the extreme stanines of 1, 2, 8, or 9. This means that most students taking the ISEE achieve scores in the middle ranges. Only the top 4% of all test takers receive a stanine of 9 on any given section, while 20% of students receive a stanine of 5.

So, what is a good ISEE score?

Stanine scores (which range from 1 to 9) are the most important and are the scores schools pay the most attention to. But what is a good score on the ISEE? A score of 5 or higher will be enough to put students in the running for most schools, although some elite private schools want applicants to have ISEE test results of 7 or higher.

Here's a sample ISEE Report

Individual Student Report

Candidate for Grade	8	
ID Number		
Gender	**Male**	
Date of Birth	**4/8/2004**	
Phone Number		
Test Level/Form	**Middle/0916**	
Date of Testing	**11/30/2016**	
Tracking Number	**201612010592103**	

The Test Profile below shows your total scores for each test. Refer to the enclosed brochure called *Understanding the Individual Student Report* to help you interpret the *Test Profile* and *Analysis*. Percentile Ranks and Stanines are derived from norms for applicants to independent schools.

TEST PROFILE

Section	Scaled Score (760 – 940)	Percentile Rank (1 – 99)	Stanine (1 – 9)	Stanine Analysis 1 2 3 4 5 6 7 8 9
Verbal Reasoning	895	90	8	V
Reading Comprehension	890	76	6	R
Quantitative Reasoning	894	81	7	Q
Mathematics Achievement	883	61	6	M

LEGEND: V = Verbal Reasoning R = Reading Comprehension Q = Quantitative Reasoning M = Mathematics Achievement

ANALYSIS

Section & Subsection	# of Questions	# Correct	Results for Each Question
Verbal Reasoning			
Synonyms	18	15	+++++++- ++++- ++- +
Single Word Response	17	16	+++++++++++- +++++
Quantitative Reasoning			
Word Problems	18	11	+++- - - +++- +++++- - -
Quantitative Comparisons	14	14	++++++++++++++
Reading Comprehension			
Main Idea	4	4	++++
Supporting Ideas	6	5	- +++++
Inference	6	5	+- ++++
Vocabulary	7	5	+++- +- +
Organization/Logic	4	4	++++
Tone/Style/Figurative Language	3	3	+++
Mathematics Achievement			
Whole Numbers	7	4	+- +++- -
Decimals, Percents, Fractions	9	5	++- - ++- - +
Algebraic Concepts	11	7	+++++- ++- - -
Geometry	4	2	+- +-
Measurement	5	4	++++-
Data Analysis and Probability	6	4	+++- +-

LEGEND: + = Correct   - = Incorrect   S = Skipped   N = Not Reached

The test was administered in the order reported in the analysis section; Verbal Reasoning, Quantitative Reasoning, Reading Comprehension, and Mathematics Achievement. Each section was divided into subsections, grouping similar types of questions. The Reading Comprehension subsection grouping does not represent the actual order of the test questions.

The above is a preliminary ISEE report. ERB reserves the right to amend this report before it is finalized. The report will be final no later than 20 business days. The final report will automatically be generated electronically.

ISEE—Upper Level Exam-3

Verbal Reasoning

You have 20 minutes to answer the 40 questions in the Verbal Reasoning Section.

This section is divided into two parts that contain two different types of questions. As soon as you have completed Part I, answer the questions in Part II. You may write in your test booklet. For each answer you select, fill in the corresponding circle on your answer document.

Part I—Synonyms

Each question in Part I consists of a word in capital letters followed by four answer choices. Select the one word that is most nearly the same in meaning as the word in capital letters.

SAMPLE QUESTION: Sample Answer

CHARGE: A B ● D

(A) release
(B) belittle
(C) accuse
(D) conspire

Part II—Sentence Completion

Each question in Part II is made up of a sentence with one blank. Each blank indicates that a word or phrase is missing. The sentence is followed by four answer choices. Select the word or phrase that will best complete the meaning of the sentence as a whole.

SAMPLE QUESTIONS: Sample Answer

It rained so much that the streets were _____.   ● B C D

(A) flooded
(B) arid
(C) paved
(D) crowded

The house was so dirty that it took _____.   A B C ●

(A) less than 10 min to wash it
(B) four months to demolish it
(C) over a week to walk across it
(D) two days to clean it

Part I—Synonyms

> ## Directions:
> Select the word that is most nearly the same in meaning as the word in capital letters.

1. ACRIMONIOUS:

   (A) resentful   (B) sympathetic   (C) kind   (D) sweet

2. AROMATIC:

   (A) fragrant   (B) malodorous   (C) smelly   (D) putrid

3. CONFLAGRATION:

   (A) peace   (B) inferno   (C) truce   (D) calm

4. TORPID:

   (A) active   (B) lethargic   (C) busy   (D) engaged

5. ABEYANCE:

   (A) renewal   (B) continuance   (C) suspension   (D) continuation

6. JARRING:

   (A) typical   (B) usual   (C) startling   (D) customary

7. INJURIOUS:

   (A) harmless   (B) beneficial   (C) innocuous   (D) detrimental

8. SATURNINE:

   (A) cheerful   (B) friendly   (C) bright   (D) somber

9. STAID:

   (A) humorous   (B) flippant   (C) stern   (D) playful

10. PREVARICATE:

    (A) lie (B) testify (C) assert (D) swear

11. TRITE:

    (A) novel (B) interesting (C) original (D) cliche

12. VERISIMILAR:

    (A) fake (B) realistic (C) different (D) sham

13. ABASE:

    (A) elevate (B) debauch (C) exalt (D) uplift

14. CIRCUMSPECT:

    (A) cautious (B) careless (C) reckless (D) bold

15. GLIB:

    (A) audacity (B) silence (C) humility (D) shame

16. IMPUGN:

    (A) defend (B) justify (C) advocate (D) condemn

17. PANEGYRIC:

    (A) peace (B) chaos (C) serenity (D) harmony

18. PUTREFY:

    (A) ripen (B) grow (C) rot (D) mature

19. FINICKY:

    (A) affable (B) lax (C) lenient (D) picky

20. SCURRILOUS:

    (A) respectful (B) civil (C) insulting (D) polite

Part II—Sentence Completion

Directions:

Select the word that best completes the sentence.

21. The new president had _____ suspicions that the newly elect cabinet is plotting corruption.

    (A) ripe (B) inchoate (C) mature (D) full-blown

22. Her boyfriend got tired of her _____ voice every time he can't keep up with her outrageous demands.

    (A) querulous (B) stoic (C) gentle (D) patient

23. It was rumored that President Carter bought votes to _____ his ranking which made him win the elections.

    (A) abate (B) aggrandize (C) reduce (D) diminish

24. Despite the low offer, Haren accepted the job with _____ as it was her stepping-stone to her long-term career goal.

    (A) indifference (B) reluctance (C) alacrity (D) hesitation

25. It was useless to reprimand her since she always does the _____ to what her parents or her closest friends tell her.

    (A) replica (B) copy (C) duplicate (D) antithesis

26. History books are being debunked lately for retelling _____ stories as more people claim that their ancestors have told them differently about the past.

    (A) factual (B) true (C) literal (D) apocryphal

27. Mr. Smith was ejected from the elite circle for casting _____ on the leader's right hand. He did it to uplift his status and eventually take the position over.

    (A) praise (B) commendation (C) aspersions (D) applause

28. The audience were not only _____ by the actor's charm but also by his presence on stage, his chemistry with his costar, and his talent in acting.

    (A) repelled (B) beguiled (C) offended (D) revolted

29. A crowd of men were seen unhappily leaving Lady Katrina's home as she continues to refuse to yield to their _____ and to wait for the most fitting candidate.

   (A) blandishments   (B) detraction   (C) depreciation   (D) disparagement

30. Thomas didn't bother to study for finals as he has already orchestrated his way to _____ in the exam by sneaking into the teacher's office and getting the answer sheet.

   (A) bilk   (B) honest   (C) integrity   (D) ace

31. Their family was a target of _____ for being _____. They were the only immigrants in the community.

   (A) malice ... generous   (B) praise ... popular   (C) calumny ... different   (D) remarks ... friendly

32. For his _____, Sir Richard was given the _____ of "the Mighty." He led an army and defeated the second strongest kingdom in the land.

   (A) laziness ... title   (B) looks ... nickname   (C) accomplishments ... epithet   (D) cowardy ... name

33. Mother always reminds us with a _____ "you can lead a horse to water, but you can't make him drink." In helping people, help them to be independent and do not teach them to be _____.

   (A) signage ... strong   (B) scolding ... intelligent   (C) maxim ... incapable   (D) saying ... capable

34. While what you often see in period dramas are glamour, back in the Victorian England era, many lived in _____. Some people believed that their living situation was because of laziness or because they were simply not _____ of fortune.

   (A) mansions ... born   (B) squalor ... worthy   (C) high-end ... capable   (D) wealth ... worthy

35. Joseph left Clara heartbroken for a _____ of bribe her parents _____ him to stay away from her and let her marry into a wealthy family.

   (A) drop ... obtained   (B) handful ... stopped   (C) vast ... claimed   (D) pittance ... offered

36. After several negotiations, the investors decided to _____ under three _____. They will need to change the percentage of shares, total budget cost, and agree to the same contractor.

   (A) resist ... rules   (B) contend ... orders   (C) defy ... subjects   (D) capitulate ... conditions

37. He has never been seen _____ until his _____ from the failed engagement with Eda.

   (A) dancing ... happiness   (B) carousing ... heartbreak   (C) celebrating ... heartache

   (D) enjoying ... joy

38. It always made my heart _____ seeing children _____ on the first day of summer break.

   (A) jubilant ... whining   (B) melancholic ... studying   (C) jolly ... cavorting   (D) ache ... playing

39. There is no way to _____ the company's dress code with a _____ security personnel like Sawyers.

(A) circumvent ... vigilant   (B) adhere ... strict   (C) bypass ... oblivious   (D) change ... dazed

40. Her words were _____ and there was no _____ from her persuasion. In the end, I was lured into the trap.

(A) irrelevant ... dodging   (B) cogent ... escaping   (C) doubtful ... fighting   (D) dumb ... shaking

End of section.

If you have any time left, go over the questions in this section only.

Do not start the next section.

Quantitative Reasoning

You have 35 minutes to answer the 37 questions in the Quantitative Reasoning Section.

Each question is followed by four suggested answers. Read each question and then decide which one of the four suggested answers is best.

Find the row of spaces on your document that has the same number as the question. In this row, mark the space having the same letter as the answer you have chosen. You may write in your test booklet.

EXAMPLE 1:   <u>Sample Answer</u>

What is the value of the expression $(4 + 6) \div 2$?   A   B   ●   D

(A) 2
(B) 4
(C) 5
(D) 7

The correct answer is 5, so circle C is darkened.

EXAMPLE 2:

A square has an area of 25 cm². What is the length of one of its side?   A   ●   C   D

(A) 1 cm
(B) 5 cm
(C) 10 cm
(D) 25 cm

The correct answer is 5 cm, so circle B is darkened.

Part I—Word Problems (20 QS)

Each question in Part I is consisting of a word problem followed by four answer choices. Look at the four answer choices given and select the best answer.

1. A group of friends were tasked to buy flowers for an event. Cole bought 12 flowers more than Myla. Myla bought twice more than Lenny. If they bought 82 flowers total, how many flowers did Myla bought?

(A) 28   (B) 40   (C) 14   (D) 26

2. Cass is training hard to qualify for the National Games. She has a regular weekly routine, training for 5 hr a day on some days, and 3 hr a day on the other days. She trains altogether 27 hr in a week. On how many days does she train for 5 hr?

(A) 2 days   (B) 4 days   (C) 3 days   (D) 1 day

3. A cube has a volume of 125 cm³, what is its surface area?

(A) 125 cm²   (B) 100 cm²   (C) 120 cm²   (D) 150 cm²

4. The sum of two consecutive even integers is 230. What are the integers?

(A) 110 and 112   (B) 114 and 116   (C) 112 and 114   (D) 116 and 118

5. Chen and Lily decided to go on hiking in a mountain near their town. The distance from the foot of the mountain to the top is 3,500 m. It took them 50 min to reach the top. How fast did they climb to get at the top of the mountain?

(A) 60 m/min   (B) 70 m/min   (C) 80 m/min   (D) 90 m/min

6. In a group of 120 people, 90 have an age of more 30 years, and the others have an age of less than 20 years. If a person is selected at random from this group, what is the probability the person's age is less than 20?

(A) 75%   (B) 50%   (C) 30%   (D) 25%

7. A basketball team played 32 games and won three times as many games as it lost. How many games did the team win?

(A) 24   (B) 20   (C) 8   (D) 16

8. One hundred sixty-two guests attended a banquet. Three servers provided their beverages. The second server helped three times as many people as the first server and the third server helped twice as many people as the first server. How many guests did each server help?

(A) The first server helped 25 guests; 75 guests for the second server; 62 guests for the third server.

(B) The first server helped 20 guests; 90 guests for the second server; 52 guests for the third server.

(C) The first server helped 29 guests; 72 guests for the second server; 61 guests for the third server.

(D) The first server helped 27 guests; 81 guests for the second server; 54 guests for the third server.

9. Felicia wants to buy a new toy. She saved up to $25 consisting of nickels and dimes. There are three times as many nickels as dimes. How many coins of each kind are there?

(A) 100 dimes and 300 nickels   (B) 100 dimes and 200 nickels

(C) 100 dimes and 100 nickels   (D) 100 dimes and 400 nickels

10. What is the product of 5.6500 and 2.740?

(A) 5.481   (B) 5.841   (C) 15.481   (D) 105.841

11. The ratio of blue paint to red paint to white paint needed to make a mixture of lavender paint is to 4:2:1. How many gallons of blue paint will be needed if there's 42 gallons of lavender paint?

(A) 12   (B) 24   (C) 6   (D) 18

12. Nico received $50 as a gift. He plans to buy two cassette tapes that cost $8.75 each and a headphone set that costs $20. How much money will he have left?

(A) $16.25   (B) $37.50   (C) $12.50   (D) $15.20

13. If one number is three times as large as another number and the smaller number is increased by 19, the result is 6 less than twice the larger number. What is the larger number?

(A) 15   (B) 14   (C) 13   (D) 12

14. If Oliver can type 500 pages of manuscript in 19 days, how many days will it take him to type 200 pages if he works at the same rate?

(A) 7.2 days   (B) 7.6 days   (C) 6.7 days   (D) 6.2 days

15. How much simple interest will an account earn in five years if $450 is invested at 7% interest per year?

(A) $175.05   (B) $157.05   (C) $175.50   (D) $157.50

16. If the area of a circle is 81π m², what is its circumference?

(A) 18π m   (B) 16π m   (C) 14π m   (D) 12π m

17. The sum of the angles of a triangle is 180°. The second angle is 45° more than the first angle and the third angle is also 45° more than the first angle. What are the three angles?

(A) 50°, 70°, and 70°   (B) 50°, 65°, and 65°   (C) 30°, 75°, and 75°   (D) 40°, 70°, and 70°

18. What is the value of x in the expression: $2(2x - 36 + x) = 12 - 4x$?

(A) 6.8   (B) 14   (C) 10.5   (D) 8.4

19. When eight times a number is increased by 11, the result is 139. Find the number.

(A) 15   (B) 16   (C) 17   (D) 18

20. Yolanda is 16 years younger than Krishan. If the sum of their ages is 30, how old is Yolanda?

(A) 7 years old   (B) 23 years old   (C) 14 years old   (D) 10 years

Part II—Quantitative Comparison (17 QS)

All questions in Part II are quantitative comparisons between the quantities shown in Column A and Column B. Using the information given in each question, compare the quantity in Column A to the quantity in Column B, and choose one of these four answer choices:

(A) the quantity in Column A is greater

(B) the quantity in Column B is greater

(C) the two quantities are equal

(D) the relationship cannot be determined from the information given

1.

Column A	Column B
The area of a trapezoid whose parallel sides are 12 cm and 23 cm, respectively	The height of a trapezoid

2.

Column A	Column B
$2 + 6^2 - (10 \times 2) \div 2$	28

3.

Column A	Column B
Twice a number increased by 16	$2x - (-16)$

4. Town A is 80 km due north of Town B and Town C is 75 km due west of Town B.

Column A	Column B
160 km	Shortest distance from Town A to Town C

5. A circle has a radius of 14 cm.

Column A	Column B
Circumference of the circle	Area of the circle

6.

Column A	Column B
45% of 100	55% of 80

7.

Column A	Column B
The odd number after 74	The even number before 80

8. The price of an item originally is $9.50. The price got discounted by 20%.

Column A	Column B
The new price	$7.70

9.

Column A	Column B
Distance around the triangle if each side has length of 7.2	Distance around the square if each side has length 5.4

10.

Column A	Column B
$\dfrac{2}{\sqrt{25}}$	$\dfrac{1^3}{10}$

11. The area of a rectangle is 325 in² whose length is 1 less than twice the width.

Column A	Column B
The dimensions of the square	The perimeter of the square

12. In July, grapes were selling for $350.00 per kilogram. In August, the price of grapes was 8% higher than the July price. In September, the price of grapes was 10% lower than the August price.

Column A	Column B
The price of grapes in August	The price of grapes in September

13.

Column A	Column B
$\dfrac{5}{12} + \dfrac{4}{12}$	75%

14. A two-sided coin is tossed three times and lands on "tails" each time. The coin is tossed fourth time.

Column A	Column B
30%	The probability that "tails" will be the result

15. The sum of three consecutive whole numbers is 318.

Column A	Column B
The largest of the three numbers	102

16.

Column A	Column B
$(x - y)(x^2 + xy + y^2)$	$x^3 - y^3$

17.

Column A	Column B
The average of 28, 26, 24, 22	The mode of 32, 27, 30, 21, 27

End of section.

If you have any time left, go over the questions in this section only.

Do not start the next section.

You have 35 minutes to answer the 36 questions in the Reading Comprehension and Vocabulary section.

Directions:

This section contains six short reading passages. Each passage is followed by six questions based on its content. Answer the questions following each passage on the basis of what is stated or implied in that passage. You may write in your test booklet.

Questions 1–6

New research shows Black children and adults are at higher risk of having a food allergy than various other racial and ethnic groups.

A report published Thursday by the National Center for Health Statistics estimates 7.6% of Black children 17 years old and younger had a food allergy in 2021, compared with 5.3% of white children and 5% of Hispanic children. Food allergy prevalence was 6.6% among Asian children, which researchers said was not significantly different from the prevalence among either Hispanic or white children.

Overall, about 1 in 17 children in the U.S. had a diagnosed food allergy in 2021, according to the analysis, the findings of which were based on data from the 2021 National Health Interview Survey. Prevalence was similar at 5.9% among boys compared with 5.8% of girls. A study published in 2013 pegged the economic cost related to food allergies in children in the U.S. at nearly $25 billion annually.

The prevalence of food allergies in children increased with age, with 7.1% of kids 12 to 17 years old having a food allergy in 2021, compared with 5.8% of kids 6 to 11 and 4.4% of those 5 and younger.

Similar racial or ethnic disparities in food allergies were found among adults, with a second report out Thursday showing 8.5% of Black adults had a food allergy in 2021 compared with 6.2% of white, 4.5% of Asian and 4.4% of Hispanic adults.

Overall, 6.2% of adults had a food allergy in 2021, according to the report. Nearly 8% of women had a food allergy compared with 4.6% of men. Older adults were less likely to have a food allergy: 4.5% of those 75 and older and 5.1% of those between 65 and 74 had a diagnosed food allergy in 2021, compared with 6.7% of adults 45 to 64 years old and 6.6% of adults ages 18 to 44.

1. What is the main topic of the passage?

(A) the racial disparity of the prevalence of food allergies between Black and other racial and ethnic groups

(B) data that white children are at a higher risk of food allergy compared to other racial and ethnic groups

(C) data to support lactose- and gluten-free diet to avoid food allergy

(D) more Asian children have food allergies compared to other racial and ethnic groups

2. According to the passage, is the data different with age?

(A) Yes, Black children are at higher risk while white adults are at higher risk of food allergy between the ages 18 and older.

(B) No, similar racial or ethnic disparities in food allergies were found among adults.

(C) Yes, white children 17 years old and younger are at higher risk while Black people 18 years and older are higher risk for adults.

(D) No, the data shows equal prevalence of food allergy to all racial and ethnic groups.

3. Where were the findings wherein about 1 in 17 children in the U.S. had a diagnosed food allergy from?

(A) 2021 National Health Interview Survey   (B) 2022 National Health Interview Survey

(C) National Food and Drug Association   (D) not known

4. True or false. According to the report shared on the passage, more adult women are reported to have a food allergy compared to adult men.

(A) true   (B) false   (C) maybe   (D) not stated

5. Which among the words below are synonymous with the underlined word in line 11?

(A) rareness   (B) unusualness   (C) occurrence   (D) infrequence

6. What does the underlined word in line 27 mean?

(A) a point which two or more things share

(B) the quality or state of having many qualities in common

(C) the state or fact of being the same in number, amount, status, or quality

(D) a noticeable and usually significant difference or dissimilarity

Questions 7–12

The <u>arctic</u> temperatures and gusting winds are responsible for at least one death as Friday's high winds were blamed for the death of an infant in Southwick, Massachusetts.

The winds brought a tree branch down on a vehicle driven by a 23-year-old Winsted, Connecticut, woman, according to a statement from the Hampden district attorney's office.

The driver was taken to the hospital with serious injuries, but the infant died, authorities said.

The powerful arctic blast will bring "dangerously cold wind chill temperatures" to the Northeast through Saturday evening along with blizzard conditions through northern Maine, forecasters have warned.

The Arctic air that <u>descended</u> on the Northeast on Saturday brought sub-zero temperatures and wind chills to the region, including a record-setting wind chill of minus 108 degrees Fahrenheit (minus 78 C) on the summit of Mount Washington in New Hampshire.

On Saturday, Rochester, New York matched its record low temperature of minus 8 set for this date in 1918, federal forecasters said.

According to the National Weather Service, the following cities also set record lows for Feb. 4 on Saturday: Boston; Providence, Rhode Island; Hartford, Connecticut; and Worcester, Massachusetts. The minus 10 degrees Fahrenheit temperature in Boston smashed the previous Feb. 4 record of minus 2 set in 1886. The minus 13 degrees temperature in Albany, New York, tied the record low for the date. Glens Falls, New York, set a record low of minus 24 degrees, colder than the previous record of minus 22 set in 1978.

"Temperatures will be 10 to 30 degrees below average over parts of the Northeast into the coastal mid-Atlantic," the National Weather Service said in a bulletin.

Wind chill warnings and advisories have been issued across New York state and New England, it said.

The weather service added that high winds could bring power outages and damage property over the northern Rocky Mountain front and the High Plains.

7. What is the main topic of the passage?

(A) the weather forecast and how it will be extremely cold in the areas mentioned above

(B) encourage readers to go out as it will be a warm sunny day

(C) suggestions on how to spend the summer weekend

(D) warning to stop driving with an infant

8. How was the weather involved in the death of an infant in Southwick, Massachusetts?

(A) the cold wind froze the passengers in the car including the infant

(B) there was hail and cracked open the car windows

(C) winds brought a tree branch down on a vehicle driven by a woman with an infant in the car

(D) the car got trapped in the snow for hours

9. True or false. According to passage, Glens Falls, New York, set a record low of minus 26 degrees, colder than the previous record of minus 22 set in 1981.

(A) true　(B) false　(C) maybe　(D) not stated

10. How will the high winds affect the Rocky Mountain front and the High Plains?

(A) will bring heavy rain and cause flood

(B) will bring a snowstorm and possibly stop midday

(C) nothing different than a chilly winter day

(D) will bring power outages and damage property

11. What does the underlined word in line 1 mean?

(A) having a low or subnormal temperature　(B) having to do with or suggestive of fire

(C) having or expressing great depth of feeling　(D) having or giving off heat to a moderate degree

12. Which among the words below is synonymous with the underlined word in line 16?

(A) plunged (B) climbed (C) mounted (D) arose

Questions 13–18

At the end of last year, the state of New York banned pet stores from selling cats, dogs, or rabbits. The state wants to encourage pet stores to work with shelters, rather than puppy mills, to get animals adopted. With any luck, other states will follow suit.

In her story The Ones Who Walk Away from Omelas, Ursula Le Guin described a society where the joy of its citizens depended upon the "abominable misery" of a single child immured in a dungeon. Le Guin asked the reader if even great happiness could justify suffering. Humanity's relationship to animals is predicated on a similar utilitarian calculus. Like the town of Omelas, we have made a silent pact to dominate pets for our benefit, despite the cost to the pets themselves, to wild and farmed animals, and to our own morality.

Pet ownership is bad for pets. The animals are harmed from the outset, regardless of whether they are sourced from puppy mills, the wild, or artisanal inbreeders. Often African grey parrots and other "exotics" are captured from their habitats, and many die en route to the market. Puppy mills are plagued by high mortality rates for the young, while mothers are kept perpetually pregnant until they are discarded. Pedigreed animals, whose genetics are equivalent to the offspring of siblings, are often plagued by health problems during their truncated lives.

Other harms may similarly cut a pet's life short. Dogs are often hit by vehicles, fall out of them, or bake in them. The equivalent to 6% of the American cat and dog population (8 million animals) are abandoned at shelters every year—half of whom are then killed. In some cities, the number of new shelter animals has soared as people give up their "pandemic pets."

13. What is the main topic of the passage?

(A) promoting pet ownership

(B) encouraging readers to say no to pet ownership

(C) advertising the best shops to get pets from

(D) discouraging readers from getting pets from the shelters as they are not well taken care of

14. True or false. According to the passage, pet ownership is bad for pets when they are sourced from puppy mills and pet shops. Therefore, only get pets from the shelter.

(A) true (B) false (C) maybe (D) not stated

15. How is pet ownership harmful to pets?

(A) puppy mills have high mortality rate and mothers are kept perpetually pregnant until they are discarded.

(B) other animals die en route to the market

(C) A, B, and D

(D) pedigreed animals often have health problems

16. Why was there an increase in shelter animals?

(A) because many breeders give up their extra litter

(B) because there is an increase in birth rate from existing pets

(C) because people have started giving up the pets they got during the pandemic

(D) not known

17. What is the meaning of the underlined word in line 13?

(A) as oppose with (B) contradictory to (C) unlike (D) based on

18. Which word is synonymous with the underlined word in line 27?

(A) never (B) once (C) seldom (D) always

Questions 19–24

A nine-year-old boy from Pennsylvania who loves science and computer programming has become one of the youngest ever high school graduates, and he has already started accumulating some credits toward his college degree.

David Balogun recently received a diploma from Reach cyber charter school—based in his state's capital of Harrisburg—after taking classes remotely from his family home in the Philadelphia suburb of Bensalem, the local television station WGAL reported Saturday.

The achievement makes David one of the youngest known children to ever graduate high school, according to a list compiled by the history and culture website oldest.org.

The only person on that list younger than David was Michael Kearney, who still holds the Guinness world record for youngest high school graduate that he set when he was six in 1990 before he ultimately obtained master's degrees at 14 and 18 and won more than $1m on gameshows. David would come in higher on that list than Pulitzer prize-winning journalist Ronan Farrow, who was 11 when he finished high school.

David told WGAL that he already knows which he wants to dedicate his professional life to once he completes his education.

"I want to be an astrophysicist, and I want to study black holes and supernovas," he said to the station.

David's parents both have advanced academic degrees, but they told WGAL that it is challenging to raise a child with such an <u>extraordinary</u> intellect.

"I had to get outside of the box," David's mother, Ronya, said to the outlet. "Playing pillow fights when you're not supposed to, throwing the balls in the house. He's a nine-year-old with the brain that has the capacity to understand and <u>comprehend</u> a lot of concepts beyond his years and sometimes beyond my understanding."

19. What is the main topic of the passage?

    (A) a feature about a nine-year-old boy who became one of the youngest high school graduates

    (B) a feature on the youngest high school graduate in 1990 at the age of six

    (C) what it takes to have an extraordinary child

    (D) what you need to achieve to be an astrophysicist

20. Who is the nine-year-old boy mentioned in the passage?

    (A) Michael Kearney (B) David Balogun (C) Guinness (D) Ronya

21. Who holds the record as the youngest high school graduate?

    (A) Michael Kearney (B) David Balogun (C) Guinness (D) Ronya

22. What does the nine-year-old boy want to become when he completes his education?

    (A) scientist (B) teacher (C) computer programmer (D) astrophysicist

23. What does the underlined word in line 42 mean?

    (A) to fail to attend (B) to fail to give proper attention to

    (C) to have a clear idea of (D) lack of interest or concern

24. Which is synonymous with the underlined word in line 36?

    (A) ordinary (B) exceptional (C) common (D) typical

Questions 25–30

ANKARA, Turkey—A <u>powerful</u> 7.8 magnitude earthquake hit southeast Turkey and Syria early Monday, toppling buildings, and sending panicked residents pouring outside in a cold winter night. At least 100 were killed, and the toll was expected to rise.

Rescue workers and residents frantically searched for survivors under the rubble of crushed buildings in multiple cities on both sides of the border. In one quake-struck Turkish city, dozens pulled away chunks of concrete and twisted metal. People on the street shouted up to others inside a partially toppled apartment building, leaning dangerously.

The quake, felt as far away as Cairo, was centered north of the city of Gaziantep in an area of about 60 miles from the Syrian border.

On the Syrian side of the border, the quake smashed opposition-held regions that are packed with some 4 million Syrians displaced from other parts of the country by the long civil war. Many of them live in <u>decrepit</u> conditions with little health care. At least 11 were killed in one town, Atmeh, and many more were buried in the rubble, a doctor in the town, Muheeb Qaddour, told The Associated Press by telephone.

"We fear that the deaths are in the hundreds," Qaddour said, referring to the rebel-held northwest. "We are under extreme pressure."

On the Turkish side, the area has several large cities and is home to millions of Syrian refugees.

Turkish President Recep Tayyip Erdogan said on Twitter that "search and rescue teams were immediately dispatched" to the areas hit by the quake.

"We hope that we will get through this disaster together as soon as possible and with the least damage," he wrote.

25. What is the main topic of the passage?

(A) report on the powerful earthquake that hit southeast Turkey and Syria early Monday

(B) feature of the living conditions of the Syrian refugees

(C) promotional for the president of Turkey

(D) an earthquake forecast that will hit Turkey–Syria border

26. How many people died in the earthquake?

(A) not stated   (B) 7.8   (C) 100   (D) 60

27. Which areas were hit by the 7.8 magnitude earthquake?

(A) outside the border of Turkey and Syria   (B) not stated

(C) far west of Turkey   (D) southeast Turkey and Syria

28. Who is the president of Turkey?

(A) President Atmeh   (B) President Ankara

(C) President Cairo   (D) President Recep Tayyip Erdogan

29. Which word is synonymous with the underlined word in line 1?

(A) insignificant   (B) strong   (C) weak   (D) feeble

30. What does the underlined word in line 22 mean?

(A) old and in bad condition or poor health   (B) being in an original and unused or unspoiled state

(C) having no injury, defacement, or imperfection   (D) free from dirt or stain

Questions 31–36

The bathroom consisted of a tarp tied between two trees.

When Katelyn Haruko Schmisseur used it, she made eye contact with a staff member. She squatted, they stared. A requirement of her wilderness therapy program, they told her.

Because of her eating disorder, a staff member was with her at all times almost the entire length of her stay in the Utah desert.

A bucket lined with a biohazard bag acted as a receptacle for solid waste. As the weather got warmer, the smell got stronger. The flies were incessant.

With only one roll of toilet paper a week to be split among 10 people, Katelyn would resort to cleaning herself with sticks and leaves.

"It was just so nasty," she says. "They didn't care. ... (It was) just another form of dehumanizing you and taking away your dignity."

She was 16 when she first arrived with only a few items, all stuffed into a 40-pound backpack.

The first activity? A grueling 3-mile hike.

"I was terrified," says Katelyn, now 21. "I missed my family more than anything. I just remember feeling so helpless. It's like you're living in this existence, but you don't have free will, you don't have autonomy, and they make that very clear to you. They make it very clear to you that you are a patient. You have no freedom. You have no choice."

Katelyn is one of many former campers coming forward to share their experiences with wilderness therapy, a type of treatment parents often turn to when they feel they need professional help for their kids and counseling isn't enough.

In recent years, the "troubled teen industry," which includes reform schools and residential treatment facilities, has come under scrutiny as former students speak out about the alleged mistreatment they experienced. (One big name who has elevated the cause is Paris Hilton.) But as the industry overall inches toward reform, wilderness therapy tends to fly under the radar.

31. What is the main topic of passage?

(A) feature of a teenager's experience with wilderness therapy

(B) introduce a new kind of therapy

(C) convince readers to start wilderness therapy

(D) report on the success rate of wilderness therapy

32. What condition was mentioned in the passage that Katelyn Haruko Schmisseur had which probably was one of the reasons she attended wilderness therapy?

(A) anger management issue   (B) alcohol dependent   (C) substance abuse   (D) eating disorder

33. How does Katelyn describe her experience with the wilderness therapy?

(A) she felt that she belonged since everybody was friendly

(B) she felt mistreated and lacked autonomy

(C) she felt recovered from her troubles

(D) she had fun with her exposure to nature

34. What does the underlined word in line 13 mean?

(A) going on and on without any interruptions

(B) appearing or occurring repeatedly from time to time

(C) occurring or appearing at intervals

(D) lacking in steadiness or regularity of occurrence

35. Which among the words below is a synonym of the underlined word in line 40?

(A) glance   (B) glimpse   (C) inspection   (D) peek

36. Which among the words below is an antonym of the underlined word in line 23?

(A) challenging   (B) rigorous   (C) demanding   (D) effortless

End of section.

If you have any time left, go over the questions in this section only.

Do not start the next section.

You have 40 minutes to answer the 47 questions in the Mathematics Achievement Section.

Each question is followed by four suggested answers. Read each question and then decide which one of the four suggested answers is best.

Find the row of spaces on your document that has the same number as the question. In this row, mark the space having the same letter as the answer you have chosen. You may write in your test booklet.

SAMPLE QUESTION: Sample Answer

Which of the numbers below is not factor of 364?   A ● C D

(A) 13
(B) 20
(C) 26
(D) 91

The correct answer is 20, so circle B is darkened.

---

1. A student chose a number, multiplied it by 2, then subtracted 138 from the result and got 102. What was the number he chose?

   (A) 102   (B) 120   (C) 125   (D) 105

2. Jacob works at the local pizza parlor. When he works overtime, he earns $1\frac{1}{4}$ times the normal rate. One week Jacob worked for 40 hr at the normal rate of pay and worked 12 hr overtime. If Jacob earned $660 altogether in that week, what is his normal rate of pay?

   (A) $12 per hour   (B) $16 per hour   (C) $13 per hour   (D) $17 per hour

   For questions 3–6, please refer to the problem below:

   The distance between stations A and B is 148 km. An express train left station A toward station B with the speed of 80 km/hr. At the same time, a freight train left station B toward station A with the speed of 36 km/hr. They met at station C, which is in the middle of station A and B, at 12 p.m., and by that time the express train stopped at intermediate station for 10 min and the freight train stopped for 5 min. Find:

3. The distance between stations C and B.

   (A) 48 km   (B) 100 km   (C) 52 km   (D) 38 km

4. The distance between stations A and C.

   (A) 48 km   (B) 100 km   (C) 52 km   (D) 38 km

5. The time when the freight train left station B.

(A) 10:25 a.m.   (B) 10:00 a.m.   (C) 10:35 a.m.   (D) 10:30 a.m.

6. The time when the express train left station A.

(A) 1   (B) 16   (C) 17   (D) 18

7. There are 24 students in a seventh-grade class. They decided to plant birches and roses at the school's backyard. While each girl planted three roses, every three boys planted one birch. By the end of the day, they planted 24 plants. How many birches and roses were planted?

(A) 12 roses and 12 birches   (B) 6 roses and 18 birches   (C) 18 roses and 12 birches

(D) 18 roses and 6 birches

8. Which expression has an answer of 18?

(A) $2 \times 5 + 4$ (B) $2 \times (4 + 5)$ (C) $5 \times (2 + 4)$ (D) $4 \times 2 + 5$

9. The length of a rectangle is four times its width. If the area is 100 m² what is the length of the rectangle?

(A) 15 m   (B) 5 m   (C) 17 m   (D) 20 m

10. Find an equation of the line containing (–4,5) and perpendicular to the line $5x - 3y = 4$.

(A) $3x + 5y = 13$ (B) $5x + 3y = 13$ (C) $3x - 5y = 13$ (D) $3x + 5y = -13$

11. If $a^2 + b^2 = 73$ and $2ab = 22$, what is the value of $(a - b)^2$?

(A) 31   (B) 21   (C) 51   (D) 41

12. A square measures 16 cm on one side. How much will the area be increased if the length is increased by 4 cm and the width will be decreased by 2 cm?

(A) 20 sq. cm   (B) 24 sq. cm   (C) 14 sq. cm   (D) 12 sq. cm

13. Which value is NOT equal to $\frac{6}{15}$?

(A) $\frac{2}{5}$ (B) 0.4   (C) $\frac{3}{5}$ (D) 40%

14. White gold is an alloy that was originally developed to imitate platinum (a naturally white metal). White gold consists of gold, nickel, and zinc in a ratio of 3:1:1. If an object is made of this alloy that weighs 250 g, how many grams of gold does it contain? Assuming there's no residue in making that object.

(A) 150 g   (B) 50 g   (C) 75 g   (D) 100 g

15. Solve for the value of k: $k^2 + 13 = 94$.

(A) ± 6   (B) ± 7   (C) ± 8   (D) ± 9

16. If a plane travels 1,800 miles in 7 hr 30 min, what is its average speed in miles per hour?

    (A) 225 mph   (B) 210 mph   (C) 200 mph   (D) 240 mph

17. Cleo and her four friends conducted a fund-raising event to help people that suffered from the recent storm. They were able to raise $790 total donation. She raised 35% of the total amount. What was the amount raised by the other four people?

    (A) $531.50   (B) $513.50   (C) $153.50   (D) $315.50

18. With a 21% discount, Rod was able to save $13.23 on a sweater. What was the original price of the sweater?

    (A) $63.00   (B) $49.77   (C) $13.23   (D) $53.00

19. Find the area of a circle whose diameter is 38 cm.

    (A) $1,444\pi$ sq. cm   (B) 324π sq. cm   (C) 361π sq. cm   (D) 360π sq. cm

20. Simplify: $45 \div 3^2 + (-12 + 27) - 8$

    (A) 36   (B) 12   (C) 57   (D) 40

21. One-third of the number of people attending a basketball game were admitted at a discounted price of admission. How many people paid full price if the gate receipts were $57,600.00 total?

    (A) 10,100 people   (B) 9,750 people   (C) 7, 600 people

    (D) It cannot be determined by the information given.

    For questions 22–25, please refer to the table below:

MOVIE THEATER ADMISSION
Adults: $7.50
Children (under 13): $4.00
Matinee (before 7 p.m.): $3.00

22. William (age 12) accompanied by his cousin Louise (age 15) went to see an 8:00 p.m. show. How much did they pay for the tickets?

    (A) $11.50   (B) $10.50   (C) $11.00   (D) $10.00

23. Pat took her three children and their friends to her favorite matinee. She wants to share with them how amazing the show is. If each of her children brought one friend, how much does their ticket cost?

    (A) $21.00   (B) $18.00   (C) $12.00   (D) $20.00

24. Penelope and Scott, a newlywed couple decided to watch a late-night movie in the theater. How much was their tickets?

(A) $7.50 (B) $20.00 (C) $15.00 (D) $10.00

25. Joe got a coupon with 20% discount for the movie he was eager to watch. He took his friend with him to watch this movie and he used the coupon to get a discount for himself. Both are 21 years old. How much did they pay for both tickets?

(A) $9.00 (B) $15.00 (C) $13.50 (D) $15.30

26. If $GH + 17 = 171$, and $G = 14$, then what is the value of H?

(A) 8 (B) 11 (C) 14 (D) 17

27. Ken wants to make badges from a ribbon. How many yards of ribbon will he need if he wants to make 30 badges if each badge uses 6 in of ribbon?

(A) 2 yards (B) 3 yards (C) 4 yards (D) 5 yards

28. Eric is currently working in an engineering company. It was recorded that approximately 12 fatal accidents were sustained in the company from the time it was built 20 years ago. There were approximately two nonfatal injuries to each fatal injury. What is the approximate number of nonfatal accidents recorded?

(A) 12 (B) 24 (C) 36 (D) 48

29. A section of pavement that is 9 ft long and 4 ft wide contains how many square feet?

(A) 36 sq. ft (B) 24 sq. ft (C) 30 sq. ft (D) 20 sq. ft

30. What is the value of x when $32x = 145 \times 97 \times 103 \times 82 \times 0$?

(A) 0 (B) 1 (C) 320 (D) 51

31. Mr. Medina borrowed $2,000 in a bank to start a business. If there will be 12% simple interest for two years, then what would the total interest charge be?

(A) $150.00 (B) $450.00 (C) $120.00 (D) $480.00

32. Gladys went camping with her best friend. They set up a tent for them to sleep on. What would be the surface area of the tent if it is 6 m long, 3 m wide, and 2 m high?

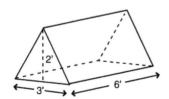

(A) 20 sq. m (B) 18 sq. m (C) 36 sq. m (D) 30 sq. m

33. Lawrence ordered some office supplies and currently sorting out the items to have it delivered on the designated departments. She has 400 reams of paper. Department 1 needs $\frac{1}{3}$ of the said supply, Department 2 needs $\frac{1}{6}$, and Department 3 needs $\frac{1}{4}$. After delivering to those three departments, how many reams of paper were left?

    (A) 133 reams   (B) 100 reams   (C) 67 reams   (D) 200 reams

34. In the figure below, the sides of ΔABC are, respectively, parallel to the sides of ΔDEF. If the complement of A is 50°, what is the complement of D?

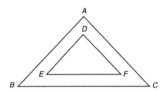

    (A) 45°   (B) 55°   (C) 50°   (D) 40°

35. If 3 pints of water are needed to water each square foot of lawn, then what is the minimum gallons of water needed for a lawn that is 12 ft long and 8 ft wide?

    (A) 18 gallons   (B) 24 gallons   (C) 36 gallons   (D) 48 gallons

36. In a bag, there are red, green, black, and white marbles. If there are 6 red, 8 green, 4 black, and 12 white marbles, and one marble is to be selected at random, what is the probability it will be white?

    (A) 40%   (B) 35%   (C) 30%   (D) 25%

37. In the expression, $(3 + 2) (6 - 2) (7 + 1) = (4 + 4) (z)$, what is the value of z?

    (A) 17   (B) 18   (C) 19   (D) 20

38. Divide: $\frac{5}{9} \div \frac{2}{6}$

    (A) $1\frac{2}{3}$ (B) $1\frac{2}{9}$ (C) $1\frac{1}{3}$ (D) $1\frac{1}{2}$

39. Miko had a birthday party and spent $11.97 on a cake, $18.51 on balloons, $16.23 on ice cream, and $12.00 on invitations. How much did Miko spend on the party?

    (A) $58.17   (B) $58.71   (C) $85.71   (D) $85.17

40. What is 140% of 45?

    (A) 62   (B) 63   (C) 64   (D) 65

41. A $395 television is on sale for 20% off. What is the sale price?

    (A) $361   (B) $163   (C) $316   (D) $136

42. Christine spends two days a week painting houses and three days a week doing carpentry. If she earns $300 a day for painting and $240 a day for carpentry, how much does she earn in a week?

(A) $1,320   (B) $1,230   (C) $1,203   (D) $1,302

43. If $\dfrac{3}{16} = \dfrac{a}{48}$, what is the value of a?

(A) 9   (B) 10   (C) 11   (D) 12

44. In the figure below, the two outer rays form a right angle. If angle 1 measures 68°, what is the measure of angle 2?

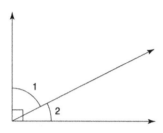

(A) 68°   (B) 20°   (C) 26°   (D) 22°

45. Which of the following numbers is evenly divisible by 4?

(A) 4,123,214   (B) 5,407,790   (C) 1,397,250   (D) 3,741,628

46. Which of the following is divisible only by itself and 1?

(A) 17   (B) 34   (C) 81   (D) 25

47. What are all the common factors of 24 and 36?

(A) 1, 2, 3, 12, 18   (B) 1, 2, 4, 12, 18, 24   (C) 1, 2, 12, 18, 24, 36   (D) 1, 2, 3, 4, 6, 12

End of section.

If you have any time left, go over the questions in this section only.

Do not start the next section.

ANSWER KEY

Verbal Reasoning

1. A	7. D	13. B	19. D	25. D	31. C	37. B
2. A	8. D	14. A	20. C	26. D	32. C	38. C
3. B	9. C	15. C	21. B	27. C	33. B	39. A
4. B	10. A	16. D	22. A	28. B	34. B	40. B
5. C	11. D	17. B	23. B	29. A	35. D	
6. C	12. B	18. C	24. C	30. A	36. D	

ISEE UL Verbal 1

1. The correct answer is (A). Acrimonious means angry and bitter, caustic, biting, or rancorous especially in feeling, language, or manner.

2. The correct answer is (A). Aromatic means having a noticeable and pleasant smell: fragrant.

3. The correct answer is (B). Conflagration means a destructive burning or a state of armed violent struggle between states, nations, or groups.

4. The correct answer is (B). Torpid means sluggish in functioning or acting.

5. The correct answer is (C). Abeyance is a state of temporary inactivity.

6. The correct answer is (C). Jarring means having a harshly concussive, disagreeable, or discordant effect. Synonyms are startling, shocking, and surprising.

7. The correct answer is (D). Injurious means inflicting or tending to inflict injury.

8. The correct answer is (D). Saturnine means of a gloomy or surly disposition.

9. The correct answer is (C). Staid is defined as marked by settled sedateness and often prim self-restraint.

10. The correct answer is (A). To prevaricate is to deviate from the truth.

11. The correct answer is (D). Trite means hackneyed or boring from much use, not fresh or original.

12. The correct answer is (B). Verisimilar means having the appearance of truth.

13. The correct answer is (B). To abase means to lower in rank, office, prestige, or esteem or to lower physically.

14. The correct answer is (A). Circumspect means careful to consider all circumstances and consequences.

15. The correct answer is (C). Glib means showing little forethought or preparation, marked by ease and informality.

16. The correct answer is (D). To impugn means to assail by words or arguments: oppose or attack as false or lacking integrity.

17. The correct answer is (B). A panegyric is a formal or elaborate praise.

18. The correct answer is (C). To putrefy means to undergo destructive dissolution. It implies the rotting of animal matter and offensiveness to sight and smell.

19. The correct answer is (D). Finicky means hard to please.

20. The correct answer is (C). Scurrilous means using or given to coarse language, vulgar and evil, or containing obscenities, abuse, or slander.

21. The correct answer is (B). Inchoate means being only partly in existence or operation. In this sentence, the president has a hunch that the newly elect cabinet is planning corruption which means it has not commenced yet neither proven.

22. The correct answer is (A). Querulous means habitually complaining, fretful, whining. In this sentence, the subject can't keep up with his girlfriend's whining whenever her demands are not met.

23. The correct answer is (B). To aggrandize is to make great or greater. It also means to enhance the power, wealth, position, or reputation of. In this sentence, it was rumored that President Carter bought votes to boost his ranking in the elections which made him win.

24. The correct answer is (C). Alacrity means promptness in response: cheerful readiness.

25. The correct answer is (D). Antithesis means the direct opposite.

26. The correct answer is (D). Apocryphal is of doubtful authenticity: spurious.

27. The correct answer is (C). Aspersion means a false or misleading charge meant to harm someone's reputation.

28. The correct answer is (B). To beguile means to engage the interest of by or as if by guile. It also means to lead by deception.

29. The correct answer is (A). Blandishment means something that tends to coax or cajole. Synonyms are seduction, charm, and flattery.

30. The correct answer is (A). To bilk means to cheat out of something valuable.

31. The correct answer is (C). Calumny is the act of uttering false charges or misrepresentations maliciously calculated to harm another's reputation. In this sentence, the subject was a target or malice/calumny for being the only immigrant in the community which makes them different from the rest.

32. The correct answer is (C). Epithet is a descriptive or familiar name given instead of or in addition to the one belonging to an individual. It can either be good or bad. In this sentence, Sir Richard was awarded the nickname "the Mighty" for winning the battle against the second strongest kingdom in the land.

33. The correct answer is (B). A maxim is a proverbial saying. In this sentence, the speaker remembers his mother's reminder of a proverbial saying when helping other people.

34. The correct answer is (B). Squalor refers to awfully bad and dirty conditions. In this sentence, there were many people who lived in squalor behind the glamour one sees from period dramas.

35. The correct answer is (D). Pittance means an exceedingly small sum of money. In this sentence, Joseph was bribed by Clara's parents with a small amount and left Clara heartbroken.

36. The correct answer is (D). To capitulate means to surrender often after negotiation of terms. In this sentence, the investors finally decided to agree after several negotiations under three conditions.

37. The correct answer is (B). To carouse means to take part in drunken revelry. In this sentence, the subject has never been seen drinking until his recent heartbreak from the failed engagement.

38. The correct answer is (C). To cavort means to play and run about happily.

39. The correct answer is (A). To circumvent is to avoid having to comply with (something) especially through cleverness.

40. The correct answer is (B). Cogent means having the power to persuade.

Quantitative Reasoning

WORD PROBLEMS		QUANTITATIVE COMPARISONS	
1. A	11. B	1. D	11. D
2. C	12. C	2. C	12. A
3. D	13. A	3. C	13. C
4. B	14. B	4. A	14. B
5. B	15. D	5. B	15. A
6. D	16. A	6. A	16. C
7. A	17. C	7. B	17. B
8. D	18. D	8. B	
9. A	19. B	9. C	
10. C	20. A	10. A	

Part I—Word Problems (20 QS)

1. Answer: **A**

   Let x be the number of flowers Lenny bought, $2x$ for the flowers Myla bought and $2x + 12$ for the flowers Cole bought. Add the flowers they bought: $x + 2x + 2x + 12 = 82 \implies 5x = 82 + 12 \implies 5x = 70 \implies x = 14$. So, Lenny bought 14 flowers and since Myla bought twice, substitute the 14 in the value of x: $2(14) = 28$, hence the answer is A.

2. Answer: **C**

   Let x be the number of days she trains for 5 hr, and y be the days she trains for 3 hr. There are seven days in a week, so we can add: $x + y = 7$. It was also indicated that she trains a total of 27 hr a week, so we can add $5x + 3y = 27$. Let's solve for by substituting $x + y = 7 \implies y = 7 - x$ to the expression: $5x + 3y = 27 \implies 5x + 3(7 - x) = 27 \implies 5x + 21 - 3x = 27 \implies 2x = 6 \implies x = 3$. Cass trains 5 hr in a day, three days a week, hence the answer is C.

3. Answer: **D**

   To solve for the volume of a cube, use the formula $V = s^3 \implies 125 = s^3 \implies s = 5$ cm. We now have the length of each side. To get the surface area of a cube, use the formula: $SA = 6s^2 = 6(5)^2 = 150$. The surface area is 150 cm², hence the answer is D.

4. Answer: **B**

   Let x be the first number, $x + 2$ for the second number. Add: $x + x + 2 = 230 \implies 2x = 228 \implies x = 114$, $x + 2 = 114 + 2 = 116$. The two numbers are 114 and 116, hence the answer is B.

5. Answer: **B**

    To solve for the speed, use the formula: Speed = Distance/Time = 3,500 m/50 min = 70 m/min. Their speed is 70 m/min, hence the answer is B.

6. Answer: **D**

    The number of people whose age is less than 20 years old is given by 120 – 90 = 30. The probability that a person selected at random from the group that is less than 20 years is given $\frac{30}{120}$ = 0.25 = 25%, hence the answer is D.

7. Answer: **A**

    Let x be the number of times they lost and $3x$ be the times that they won. $3x + x = 32 \Rightarrow 4x = 32 \Rightarrow x = 8$, they lost eight times. Substitute the value of x to get the number of times they won: 3(8) = 24. They won 24 times, hence the answer is A.

8. Answer: **D**

    Let x be the number of guests the first server assisted, $3x$ for the second server, and $2x$ for the third server. There are 162 guests total. $x + 3x + 2x = 162 \Rightarrow 6x = 162 \Rightarrow x = 27$. Substitute the value of x to get the number of guests for the second and third servers. $3x = 3(27) = 81$, $2x = 2(27) = 54$. Each server helped 27, 81, 54 guests, hence the answer is D.

9. Answer: **A**

    Let x be the number of dimes and $3x$ be the number of nickels. It is given that 1 dime is equal to 10 cents, 1 nickel is equal to 5 cents, and 1 dollar is equal to 100 cents. Solve for x: $10x + 5(3x) = 2,500 \Rightarrow 10x + 15x = 2,500 \Rightarrow 25x = 2,500 \Rightarrow x = 100$, $3x = 3(100) = 300$. There are 100 dimes and 300 nickels, hence the answer is A.

10. Answer: **C**

    Multiply: 5.650 × 2.740 = 15.481, hence the answer is C.

11. Answer: **B**

    Let x be the number of gallons. $4x + 2x + 1x = 42 \Rightarrow 7x = 42 \Rightarrow x = 6$. 4(6) = 24. Twenty-four gallons of blue paint is needed, hence the answer is B.

12. Answer: **C**

    There are two cassette tapes that cost $8.75 each, so multiply: 2(8.75) = $17.50. Add then the amount for the headphone set: $17.50 + $20.00 = $37.50. Subtract the total amount of the items from $50: $50 – $37.50 = $12.50. He has $12.50 left, hence the answer is C.

13. **Answer: A**

Let x be the smaller number, $3x$ be the larger number. Solve for x: $x + 19 = 2(3x) - 6 \implies x + 19 = 6x - 6 \implies -5x = -25$ $x = 5$. The smaller number is 5. Substitute the value of x in $3x$ to get the value of the larger number: $3x = 3(5) = 15$, hence the answer is A.

14. **Answer: B**

Let x be the number of days Oliver needs to type 200 pages. To solve, set up a proportion. We may use $\frac{\text{pages}}{\text{days}} = \frac{\text{pages}}{\text{days}} \implies \frac{500}{19} = \frac{200}{x} \implies 500x = 3,800 \implies x = 7.6$ days. It will take 7.6 days for Oliver to finish 200 pages, hence the answer is B.

15. **Answer: D**

To solve for the simple interest, use the formula: Interest(I) = principal amount $\times$ rate $\times$ time. $I = \$450\,(0.07)\,(5) = \$157.50$. The simple interest is \$157.50, hence the answer is D.

16. **Answer: A**

To solve for the area of a circle, use the formula: $A = \pi r^2$. We need to get the value of the radius(r): $81\pi = \pi r^2 \implies r^2 = 81 \implies r = 9$. Now that we have the value of the radius, use the formula: $C = 2\pi r$ to get the circumference. $C = 2\pi(9) = 18\pi$. The circumference is 18π m, hence the answer is A.

17. **Answer: C**

Let x be the first angle, $x + 45$ for the second and third angles. Solve for x: $x + x + 45 + x + 45 = 180 \implies 3x + 90 = 180 \implies 3x = 90 \implies x = 30$. Substitute the value of x to get the second and third angles: $30 + 45 = 75$. The angles are $30°$, $75°$, and $75°$, hence the answer is C.

18. **Answer: D**

Solve for x: $2(2x - 36 + x) = 12 - 4x \implies 2(3x - 36) = 12 - 4x \implies 6x - 72 = 12 - 4x \implies 10x = 84 \implies x = 8.4$. The value of x is 8.4, hence the answer is D.

19. **Answer: B**

Let x be the number. $8x + 11 = 139 \implies 8x = 128 \implies x = 16$. The number is 16, hence the answer is B.

20. **Answer: A**

Let x be Krishan's age, $x - 16$ be Yolanda's age: $x + x - 16 = 30 \implies 2x = 46 \implies x = 23$. Krishan is 23 years old. Substitute the value of x to get Yolanda's age: $23 - 16 = 7$ years old, hence the answer is A.

Part II—Quantitative Comparisons (17 QS)

1. **Answer: D**

    There's not enough data to get the area of trapezoid. We only have the dimensions of the bases, hence the answer is D.

2. **Answer: C**

    To evaluate the expressions, apply the PEMDAS rule. Solve first the parenthesis and exponent: 2 + 36 – (20) ÷ 2, then do multiplication and division from left to right 2 + 36 – 10. Finally, add and subtract from left to right: 38 – 10 = 28. Both columns have the same value, hence the answer is C.

3. **Answer: C**

    Write the algebraic expression of the given problem in Column A: $2x + 16$. For Column B, distribute –1 to get $2x + 16$. Both columns have the same expression, hence the answer is C.

4. **Answer: A**

    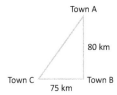

    The distance from Town A to Town C is a hypotenuse of $\triangle ABC$. To solve for the hypotenuse, use the formula: $c = \sqrt{a^2 + b^2} = \sqrt{80^2 + 75^2} = \sqrt{12,025}$ 109.65 km. Column A is greater than 109.65 km, hence the answer is A.

5. **Answer: B**

    To solve the circumference of a circle, use the formula: $C = 2\pi r = 2\pi(14) = 28\pi$. For the area, use the formula: $A = \pi r^2 = \pi(14)^2 = 196\pi$. The area is greater than the circumference, hence the answer is B.

6. **Answer: A**

    Solve the percentage: $\frac{45}{100} \times 100 = 45$; $\frac{55}{100} \times 80 = 44$. Forty-five is greater than 44, hence the answer is A.

7. **Answer: B**

    The odd number after 74 is 75. The even number before 80 is 78. Seventy-eight is greater than 74, hence the answer is B.

8. Answer: **B**

   To get the discounted/new price, multiply the original amount with the discount percentage then subtract the result from the original price: $9.50 \times \dfrac{20}{100} = 1.9 \implies \$9.50 - \$1.90 = \$7.60$. The discounted/new price is \$7.60 which is less than \$7.70, hence the answer is B.

9. Answer: **C**

   The perimeter of the triangle is $P = 3s$, while the perimeter of a square is $P = 4s$. Solve for the perimeter of both figures. $P = 3(7.2) = 21.6$; $P = 4(5.4) = 21.6$. Both columns have the same perimeter, hence the answer is C.

10. Answer: **A**

    Simplify: $\dfrac{2}{\sqrt{25}} = \dfrac{2}{5} = 0.4$; $\dfrac{1^3}{10} = \dfrac{1}{10} = 0.1$. 0.4 is greater than 0.1, hence the answer is A.

11. Answer: **D**

    The given dimensions are for a rectangle and what were asked are the dimensions of a square. A square could also be a rectangle but there's a condition that the length is 1 less than twice the width. A square has four equal sides, so we cannot use the given dimensions to get the perimeter of the square. There's not enough data given, hence the answer is D.

12. Answer: **A**

    To get the new price of the grapes for the month of August, multiply the original amount with the increase in percentage then add the result from the original price $\$350.00 \times \dfrac{8}{100} = \$28$ $\$350.00 + \implies$ $\$28.00 = \$378$. To get the price for the month of September, multiply the amount from the month of August with the decrease in percentage then subtract the result from the August price $\$378.00 \times \dfrac{10}{100} =$ $\$37.80 \implies \$378.00 - \$37.80 = \$340.20$. The price of grapes in August is higher than September, hence the answer is A.

13. Answer: **C**

    To add like terms (same denominator), simply add the values of the numerator $\dfrac{5}{12} + \dfrac{4}{12} = \dfrac{9}{12}$ or $\dfrac{3}{4}$. $\dfrac{3}{4} \times 100 = 0.75$ or 75%. Column A has the same percentage with Column B, hence the answer is C.

14. Answer: **B**

    A coin has two faces, and you will only either get "heads" or "tails." The probability of getting either "heads" or "tails" is 50%. Fifty percent is greater than 30%, hence the answer is B.

15. Answer: **A**

Let x be the smallest number and since the numbers are consecutive, we can express the second number as $x + 1$ and the third number as $x + 2$. Add: $x + x + 1 + x + 2 = 318 \implies 3x + 3 = 318 \implies 3x = 315 \implies x = 105$. The smallest number is 105, substitute this value to get the largest number: $105 + 2 = 107$. One hundred and seven is greater than 102, hence the answer is A.

16. Answer: **C**

Cubic polynomials can be solved in the similar manner as quadratic equations, where we can expand $x^3 - y^3$ and combine like terms, but to make it to a much simpler form, we can use this special product rule: Difference of the cubes: $a^3 - b^3 = (a - b)(a^2 + ab + b^2)$. $x^3 - y^3$ can be written as $(x - y)(x^2 + xy + y^2)$. Both columns have the same value, hence the answer is C.

17. Answer: **B**

To get the average of a data set, add all the numbers of the set and divide the sum to the total number of the given data of that set. $\dfrac{28 + 26 + 24 + 22}{4} = \dfrac{100}{4} = 25$. The mode is the most frequent number or the data that occurs the highest number of times. In the set in Column B, 27 is the most frequent, so the mode is 27. Twenty-seven is greater than 25, hence the answer is B.

Reading Comprehension and Vocabulary

1. A	7. A	13. B	19. A	25. A	31. A
2. B	8. C	14. B	20. B	26. C	32. D
3. A	9. B	15. C	21. A	27. D	33. B
4. A	10. D	16. C	22. D	28. D	34. A
5. C	11. A	17. D	23. C	29. B	35. C
6. D	12. A	18. D	24. B	30. A	36. D

1. The correct answer is (A). See lines 1–4. The passage shares data on new research showing that Black children and adults are at higher risk of having a food allergy than various other racial and ethnic groups.

2. The correct answer is (B). See lines 30–36.

3. The correct answer is (A). See lines 14–17.

4. The correct answer is (A). See lines 34–36. Nearly 8% of women had a food allergy compared with 4.6% of men.

5. The correct answer is (C). Prevalence is the degree to which something is prevalent. Synonyms are frequency, occurrence, and incidence.

6. The correct answer is (D). Disparity means a noticeable and usually significant difference or dissimilarity. Synonyms are difference, diversity, and discrepancy.

7. The correct answer is (A). The passage was a weather report and the States mentioned will be expecting dangerously cold wind chill temperatures.

8. The correct answer is (C). See lines 5–8.

9. The correct answer is (B). See lines 33–36. Glens Falls, New York, set a record low of minus 24 degrees, colder than the previous record of minus 22 set in 1978.

10. The correct answer is (D). See lines 44–47.

11. The correct answer is (A). Arctic means having a low or subnormal temperature. Synonyms are frigid, chilly, and icy.

12. The correct answer is (A). Descended means to lead or extend downward. Synonyms are fell, plunged, and sank.

13. The correct answer is (B). The passage is about how pet ownership has harmed pets regardless of whether they are sourced from puppy mills, the wild, or artisanal in-breeders. See line 19.

14. The correct answer is (B). False. See lines 19–22. Pet ownership is bad for pets. The animals are harmed from the outset, regardless of whether they are sourced from puppy mills, the wild, or artisanal in-breeders.

15. The correct answer is (C). See lines 22–34.

16. The correct answer is (C). See lines 37–39.

17. The correct answer is (D). To predicate something on means to assert to be a quality, attribute, or property or base on.

18. The correct answer is (D). Perpetually means for all time.

19. The correct answer is (A). See lines 1–6.

20. The correct answer is (B). See line 7.

21. The correct answer is (A). See line 18.

22. The correct answer is (D). See line 30.

23. The correct answer is (C). To comprehend means to have a clear idea of. Synonyms are to understand, decipher, and grasp.

24. The correct answer is (B). Extraordinary means being out of the ordinary. Synonyms are exceptional, unique, and remarkable.

25. The correct answer is (A). See lines 1–6.

26. The correct answer is (C). See lines 5–6.

27. The correct answer is (D). See lines 1–2.

28. The correct answer is (D). See line 33.

29. The correct answer is (B). Powerful means having great power or influence. Synonyms are strong, influential, and significant.

30. The correct answer is (A). Decrepit means fallen into ruin or disrepair. Synonyms are dilapidated, broken-down, and debilitated.

31. The correct answer is (A). See lines 32–34. Katelyn shared her experience with wilderness therapy.

32. The correct answer is (D). See line 7.

33. The correct answer is (B). Katelyn shared her terrible experience from the bathroom situation, the grueling hike, and making her feel that she is indeed a patient.

34. The correct answer is (A). Incessant means going on and on without any interruptions.

35. The correct answer is (C). Scrutiny means a close look at or over someone or something to judge condition.

36. The correct answer is (D). Grueling means requiring considerable physical or mental effort. Antonyms are easy, simple, and effortless.

Mathematics Achievement

1. B	11. C	21. D	31. D	41. C
2. A	12. B	22. A	32. C	42. A
3. A	13. C	23. A	33. B	43. A
4. B	14. A	24. C	34. C	44. D
5. C	15. D	25. C	35. C	45. D
6. C	16. D	26. B	36. A	46. A
7. D	17. B	27. D	37. D	47. D
8. B	18. A	28. B	38. A	
9. D	19. C	29. A	39. B	
10. A	20. B	30. A	40. B	

1. **Answer: B**

    Let x be the number. Solve for x: $2x - 138 = 102 \implies 2x = 240 \implies x = 120$. The number is 120, hence the answer is B.

2. **Answer: A**

    Let x be the normal rate of Jacob's pay. He works 40 hr; $40x$ and earns $1\frac{1}{4}$ times the normal rate for overtime with 12 hr for the overtime that week; $12 \times 1\frac{1}{4} x$. He earned \$660 in that week so, $40x + (12 \times 1\frac{1}{4} x) = 660 \implies 40x + 15x = 660 \implies 55x = 660 \implies x = 12$. Jacob's normal rate of pay is \$12 per hour, hence the answer is A.

3. **Answer: A**

    Let x be the distance between stations B and C, the distance from station C to station A is $148 - x$. By the time of the meeting at station C, the express train has travelled $\frac{148 - x}{80}$ plus the 10 min or $\frac{10}{60}$ hr for the idle time. The freight train, on the other hand, has travelled $\frac{x}{36}$ plus 5 min or $\frac{5}{60}$ hr for the idle time. The trains left at the same time, so: $\frac{148 - x}{80} + \frac{10}{60} = \frac{x}{36} + \frac{5}{60}$. Get the common denominator of 80, 60, and 36, which is 720. $9(148 - x) + 120 = 20x + 60 \implies 1{,}332 - 9x + 120 = 20x + 60 \implies -29x = 1{,}392 \implies x = 48$. The distance between station B and station C is 48 km, hence the answer is A.

4. **Answer: B**

    Since we already have the distance from stations B and C, simply subtract the value of x from the total distance of stations A and B to get the distance from station A to station C: $148 - 48 = 100$. The distance between station A and station C is 100 km, hence the answer is B.

5. Answer: **C**

By the time of the meeting at station C, the freight train travelled $\frac{48}{36} + \frac{5}{60} = \frac{240 + 15}{180} = \frac{17}{12}$ or 1 hr and 25 min. It left station B at 12 p.m., subtract 1 hr and 25 min from 12:00 p.m. and it will be 10:35 a.m. The freight train left station B at 10:35 a.m., hence the answer is C.

6. Answer: **C**

The express train departed from station A the same time the freight train left station B. The freight train left at 10:35 a.m., so the express train also left at 10:35 a.m. The answer is C.

7. Answer: **D**

Let x be the number of roses and $24 - x$ be the number of birches planted. Each girl planted three roses, so $\frac{x}{3}$ and three boys planted one birch, so we have $3(24 - x)$. There are 24 students: $\frac{x}{3} + 3(24 - x) = 24$ $\Longrightarrow x + 9(24 - x) = 72 \Longrightarrow x + 216 - 9x = 72 \Longrightarrow -8x = -144 \Longrightarrow x = 18$. The students planted 18 roses. Substitute the value of x to get the number of birches planted; $24 - 18 = 6$ birches. So, they planted 18 roses and 6 birches, hence the answer is D.

8. Answer: **B**

Evaluate each expression using PEMDAS rule. Solve first the parentheses, then multiply and add.

For option A: $2 \times 5 + 4 = 10 + 4 = 14$

For option B: $2 \times (4 + 5) = 2 \times 9 = 18$

For option C: $5 \times (2 + 4) = 5 \times 6 = 30$

For option D: $4 \times 2 + 5 = 8 + 5 = 13$

Option B has 18 as the result, hence the answer is B.

9. Answer: **D**

Let l be the length and w be the width. To get the area of a rectangle, use the formula $A = lw$. The length is four times the width, so: $l = 4w$. $A = 4w \times w \Longrightarrow 100 = 4w^2 \Longrightarrow w^2 = 25 \Longrightarrow w = 5$. The width is 5 m. Substitute the value of the width to get the length; $4w = 4(5) = 20$. The length is 20 m, hence the answer is D.

10. Answer: **A**

First, find the slope of the line $5x - 3y = 4 \Longrightarrow -3y = -5x + 4 \Longrightarrow y = \frac{5}{3}x - \frac{4}{3}$. The slope is $\frac{5}{3}$. Let m be the slope of the line perpendicular to $5x - 3y = 4$; $m \times \frac{5}{3} = -1 \Longrightarrow m = -\frac{3}{5}$. The equation perpendicular to this line is given by $y - 5 = -\frac{3}{5}(x + 4) \Longrightarrow y = -\frac{3}{5}x + \frac{13}{5} \Longrightarrow 3x + 5y = 13$, hence the answer is A.

11. **Answer: C**

Expand the expression $(a - b)^2$; $(a - b)(a - b) = a^2 - 2ab + b^2$. Rearrange the terms, so we will have $a^2 + b^2 - 2ab$. Substitute with the given values: $73 - 22 = 51$, hence the answer is C.

12. **Answer: B**

Solve for the area of the square first, $A = s^2 = 16^2 = 256$ sq. cm. If the dimensions will be adjusted, it will become a rectangle. Let l be the length and w be the width. The length is increased by four. $16 + 4 = 20$. The width is decreased by 2; $16 - 2 = 14$. Solve for the area of the rectangle to get the difference of the two areas, $A = lw = 20 \times 14 = 280$ sq. cm. Subtract the area of the square from the area of the rectangle: $280 - 256 = 24$ sq. cm, hence the answer is B.

13. **Answer: C**

The fraction $\frac{6}{15}$ can be simplified to $\frac{2}{5}$. Its decimal value is 0.4 and its percentage value is 40%, hence the answer is C.

14. **Answer: A**

Let x be the weight of the alloy. $3x + x + x = 250 \implies 5x = 250 \implies x = 50$. Substitute the value of x to get the weight of the gold: $3(50) = 150$ g. We need 150 g of gold, hence the answer is A.

15. **Answer: D**

Solve for k: $k^2 + 13 = 94 \implies k^2 = 81 \implies k = 9$ or $k = -9$. The value of k can either be 9 or -9, hence the answer is D.

16. **Answer: D**

To get the average speed, use the formula: $\text{Speed} = \dfrac{\text{Distance}}{\text{Time}} = \dfrac{1,800}{7.5} = 240$. The average speed of the plane is 240 mph, hence the answer is D.

17. **Answer: B**

Since Cleo raised 35% of the total donation, the remaining 65% were raised by her four friends. Multiply 65% with total amount raised: $790 \times \dfrac{65}{100} = \$513.50$. So, Cleo's friends raised $513.50, hence the answer is B.

18. **Answer: A**

Let x be the original price. The discount is 21%; $\dfrac{21x}{100} = 13.23 \implies 21x = 1,323 \implies x = 63$. The original price is $63.00, hence the answer is A.

19. **Answer: C**

The formula to get the area of a circle is $A = \pi r^2$. The radius is half of the diameter; $38 \div 2 = 19$. $A = \pi (19)^2 = 361\pi$. The area of the circle is 361π sq. cm, hence the answer is C.

20. Answer: **B**

Apply the PEMDAS rule. Solve first the parenthesis and exponents first: $45 \div 9 + 15 - 8$, then multiply and divide from left to right: $5 + 15 - 8$, then add and subtract from left to right: $20 - 8 = 12$, hence the answer is B.

21. Answer: **D**

There's not enough data to get the total number of people. The original price was not given nor the discount percentage, hence the answer is D.

22. Answer: **A**

William is under 13 years old, so he will pay $4.00. As for his cousin, age 15, will have to pay $7.50. Add: $4.00 + $7.50 = $11.50. They need to pay $11.50, hence the answer is A.

23. Answer: **A**

There are seven people total: Pat, her three children, and their three friends (since each child brought one friend). The Matinee ticket costs $3.00 each. Multiply $3.00 × 7 = $21.00, hence the answer is A.

24. Answer: **C**

They're both adults, so they need to pay $7.50 each. $7.50 + $7.50 = $15.00. They need to pay $15.00, hence the answer is C.

25. Answer: **C**

Joe and his friend are both adults. Since Joe got a discount coupon, multiply the percentage with the price of the ticket: $7.50 \times \dfrac{20}{100} = \$1.50 \implies \$7.50 - \$1.50 = \$6.00$. Joe will only need to pay $6.00. Since it's only Joe that got a discount coupon, his friend still needs to pay the original price:

$6.00 + $7.50 = $13.50, hence the answer is C.

26. Answer: **B**

Substitute the value of G to get H: $14H + 17 = 171 \implies 14H = 154 \implies H = 11$, hence the answer is B.

27. Answer: **D**

Solve first the total inches needed: $30 \times 6 = 180$ in. There are 36 in. in 1 yard. $180 \div 36 = 5$.

Ken needs 5 yards of ribbon, hence the answer is D.

28. Answer: **B**

For each of the 12 fatal accidents there were 2 nonfatal injuries. To get the total number of nonfatal accidents, multiply: $12 \times 2 = 24$. There were approximately 24 nonfatal accidents, hence the answer is B.

29. Answer: **A**

We need to find the area of the section of the pavement. $A = lw = 9 \times 4 = 36$ sq. ft. The area of that section is 36 sq. ft, hence the answer is A.

30. Answer: **A**

Any value multiplied by 0 will result in 0, hence the answer is A.

31. Answer: **D**

To solve for the simple interest, use the formula: Interest(I) = principal amount × rate × time.

$I = \$2,000\ (0.12)\ (2) = \$480.00$. The simple interest is $480.00, hence the answer is D.

32. Answer: **C**

To find the surface area of a triangular prism, use the formula: $SA = lw + 3wh$. Substitute with the given dimensions: $SA = 6 \times 3 + 3 \times 3 \times 2 = 18 + 18 = 36$. The surface area is 36 sq. m, hence the answer is C.

33. Answer: **B**

Lawrence delivered $\frac{1}{3} + \frac{1}{6} + \frac{1}{4} = \frac{3}{4}$ out of the 400 reams of paper. There's $\frac{1}{4}$ left. $400 \times \frac{1}{4} = 100$. There're 100 reams of paper left, hence the answer is B.

34. Answer: **C**

If the sides are parallel, then the angles are congruent, hence the answer is C.

35. Answer: **C**

Find first the area of the lawn. $A = 12 \times 8 = 96$ sq. ft. Multiply it to the pints needed to water each square feet: $96 \times 3 = 288$. There are 8 pints in 1 gallon, so divide the total pints with 8: $288 \div 8 = 36$. The minimum gallons of water needed is 36, hence the answer is C.

36. Answer: **A**

Find first the total number of marbles: $6 + 8 + 4 + 12 = 30$. Divide the 12 white marbles with the total number of marbles to get the probability percentage: $\frac{12}{30} = 0.4$ or 40%. The probability of getting one white marble is 40%, hence the answer is A.

37. Answer: **D**

Solve for z: $(3 + 2)\ (6 - 2)\ (7 + 1) = (4 + 4)\ (z) \implies 5 \times 4 \times 8 = 8z \implies 8z = 160 \implies z = 20$. The value of z is 20, hence the answer is D.

38. Answer: **A**

When dividing fractions, invert the divisor and change the mathematical operation to multiplication: $\frac{5}{9} \times \frac{6}{2} = \frac{30}{18}$ or $1\frac{2}{3}$, hence the answer is A.

39. Answer: **B**

Add all the expenses for Miko's party: $11.97 + $18.51 + $16.23 + $12.00 = $58.71. Miko spent $58.71 for his birthday party, hence the answer is B.

40. Answer: **B**

Multiply: $45 \times \frac{140}{100} = 63$, hence the answer is B.

41. Answer: **C**

To find the discounted price, multiply the original price with the discount percentage, then subtract the result from the original price: $395 \times \frac{20}{100} = 79 \implies$ $395 – $79 = $316, hence the answer is C.

42. Answer: **A**

Christine spends two days to paint with $300 earning per day: $300 × 2 = $600. She spends three days doing carpentry with $240 earning per day: $240 × 3 = $720.00. Let's add: $600 + $720 = $1,320. She earns a total of $1,320 in a week, hence the answer is A.

43. Answer: **A**

To get the value of *a*, cross multiply: $16a = 144 \implies a = 9$, hence the answer is A.

44. Answer: **D**

Let *x* be the measure of angle 2. It's given that the two outer rays form a right angle which measures 90°. Subtract the measure of angle 1 from 90°; *x* = 90° – 68° = 22°. Angle 2 measures 22°, hence the answer is D.

45. Answer: **D**

A number is evenly divisible by 4 if the number formed by the last two digits is divisible by 4. Only option D has the last two digits divisible by 4, hence the answer is D.

46. Answer: **A**

The numbers that are divisible only by itself and 1 are called prime numbers. Out of all the choices, option A is the only prime number, hence the answer is A.

47. Answer: **D**

One way to get the factor is through listing: 24 = 1, 2, 3, 4, 6, 8, 12, 24; 36 = 1, 2, 3, 4, 6, 6, 9, 12, 18, 36. The common factors are 1, 2, 3, 4, 6, 12, hence the answer is D.

For the ISEE, the most commonly referenced score is the stanine score. Check out the four steps to calculating stanine scores.

Step 1: The Raw Score

The first step in scoring is calculating a raw score. This is quite simple.

Students receive one point for each correct answer and no points for incorrect answers or unanswered questions.

Tip: Because there is no score penalty for incorrect answers or unanswered questions, be sure to answer every single question! Answering all of the questions can only increase your chances of a higher score.

Step 2: The Scaled Score

Once a raw score has been calculated for each section, it is converted into a scaled score.

This conversion adjusts for the variation in difficulty between different tests. Thus, a lower raw score on a harder test could give you the same scaled score as a higher raw score on an easier test. This process is called equating.

The scaled score for each section ranges from 760 to 940.

Step 3: The Percentile Score

Next, the percentile score for each section is calculated.

Percentiles compare a student's scaled score to all other same-grade students from the past three years. This is important to understand because the ISEE is taken by students in a range of grades. The Upper Level ISEE, for instance, is taken by students applying to grades 9–12; however, the percentile score is based only on the performance of other students applying to the same grade. Thus, a student applying to 9th grade will not be compared to a student applying to 12th grade.

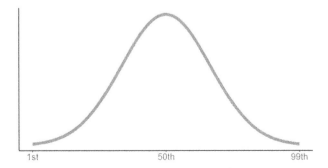

Here's an example to help understand percentile scores: scoring in the 40th percentile indicates that a student scored the same or higher than 40% of students in the same grade but lower than 59% of students.

Step 4: The Stanine Score

Finally, the percentile is converted into a stanine score.

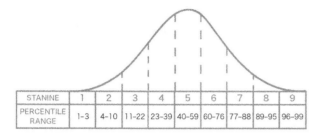

STANINE	1	2	3	4	5	6	7	8	9
PERCENTILE RANGE	1-3	4-10	11-22	23-39	40-59	60-76	77-88	89-95	96-99

Notice that the percentile ranges for the middle stanines of 4–6 are far larger than the ranges for the extreme stanines of 1, 2, 8, or 9. This means that most students taking the ISEE achieve scores in the middle ranges. Only the top 4% of all test takers receive a stanine of 9 on any given section, while 20% of students receive a stanine of 5.

So, what is a good ISEE score?

Stanine scores (which range from 1 to 9) are the most important and are the scores schools pay the most attention to. But what is a good score on the ISEE? A score of 5 or higher will be enough to put students in the running for most schools, although some elite private schools want applicants to have ISEE test results of 7 or higher.

Here's a sample ISEE Report

	Candidate for Grade	8
	ID Number	
	Gender	Male
	Date of Birth	4/8/2004
	Phone Number	
Individual Student Report	Test Level/Form	Middle/0916
	Date of Testing	11/30/2016
	Tracking Number	201612010592103

The Test Profile below shows your total scores for each test. Refer to the enclosed brochure called *Understanding the Individual Student Report* to help you interpret the *Test Profile* and *Analysis*. Percentile Ranks and Stanines are derived from norms for applicants to independent schools.

TEST PROFILE

Section	Scaled Score (760 – 940)	Percentile Rank (1 – 99)	Stanine (1 – 9)	Stanine Analysis 1 2 3 4 5 6 7 8 9
Verbal Reasoning	895	90	8	V
Reading Comprehension	890	76	6	R
Quantitative Reasoning	894	81	7	Q
Mathematics Achievement	883	61	6	M

LEGEND: V = Verbal Reasoning R = Reading Comprehension Q = Quantitative Reasoning M = Mathematics Achievement

ANALYSIS

Section & Subsection	# of Questions	# Correct	Results for Each Question
Verbal Reasoning			
Synonyms	18	15	++++++++- ++++- ++- +
Single Word Response	17	16	+++++++++++- +++++
Quantitative Reasoning			
Word Problems	18	11	+++- - - +++- +++++- - -
Quantitative Comparisons	14	14	++++++++++++++
Reading Comprehension			
Main Idea	4	4	++++
Supporting Ideas	6	5	- +++++
Inference	6	5	+- ++++
Vocabulary	7	5	+++- +- +
Organization/Logic	4	4	++++
Tone/Style/Figurative Language	3	3	+++
Mathematics Achievement			
Whole Numbers	7	4	+- +++- -
Decimals, Percents, Fractions	9	5	++- - ++- - +
Algebraic Concepts	11	7	+++++- ++- - -
Geometry	4	2	+- +-
Measurement	5	4	++++-
Data Analysis and Probability	6	4	+++- +-

LEGEND: + = Correct   - = Incorrect   S = Skipped   N = Not Reached

The test was administered in the order reported in the analysis section; Verbal Reasoning, Quantitative Reasoning, Reading Comprehension, and Mathematics Achievement. Each section was divided into subsections, grouping similar types of questions. The Reading Comprehension subsection grouping does not represent the actual order of the test questions.

The above is a preliminary ISEE report. ERB reserves the right to amend this report before it is finalized. The report will be final no later than 20 business days. The final report will automatically be generated electronically.

Ingram Content Group UK Ltd.
Milton Keynes UK
UKHW051810270623
423971UK00006B/41

9 781839 989865